SUSTAINABLE PEACE IN NORTHERN IRELAND

SUSTAINABLE PEACE IN NORTHERN IRELAND

THE ROLE OF LEADERSHIP

Sally Watson

Oxford · Berlin · Bruxelles · Chennai · Lausanne · New York

Bibliographic information published by the Deutsche Nationalbibliothek. The German National Library lists this publication in the German National Bibliography; detailed bibliographic data is available on the Internet at http://dnb.d-nb.de.

A catalogue record for this book is available from the British Library.

Library of Congress Cataloging-in-Publication Data

Names: Watson, Sally, 1951– author.
Title: Sustainable peace in Northern Ireland : the role of leadership / Sally Watson.
Description: New York : Peter Lang, [2024] | Includes bibliographical references and index.
Identifiers: LCCN 2024015317 | ISBN 9781803742915 (paperback ; acid-freepaper) | ISBN 9781803743271 (ebook) | ISBN 9781803743288 (epub)
Subjects: LCSH: Political leadership—Northern Ireland. | Peace-building—Northern Ireland. | Reconciliation—Political aspects—Northern Ireland. | Conflict management—Northern Ireland. | Northern Ireland—Social conditions—1969– | Northern Ireland—Politics and government—1998–
Classification: LCC JN1572.A91 .W38 2024 | DDC 327.1/7209416--dc23/eng/20240408
LC record available at https://lccn.loc.gov/2024015317

Cover image: © ronniejcmc.
Cover design by Peter Lang Group AG

ISBN 978-1-80374-291-5 (print)
ISBN 978-1-80374-327-1 (ePDF)
ISBN 978-1-80374-328-8 (ePub)
DOI 10.3726/b21257

© 2024 Peter Lang Group AG, Lausanne
Published by Peter Lang Ltd, Oxford, United Kingdom
info@peterlang.com - www.peterlang.com

Sally Watson has asserted her right under the Copyright, Designs and Patents Act, 1988, to be identified as Author of this Work.

All rights reserved.
All parts of this publication are protected by copyright.
Any utilisation outside the strict limits of the copyright law, without the permission of the publisher, is forbidden and liable to prosecution.
This applies in particular to reproductions, translations, microfilming, and storage and processing in electronic retrieval systems.

This publication has been peer reviewed.

In memory of my father who volunteered in 1941 to serve in the war in Europe. He was 19 years old and believed it was his duty to defend his country, and that his efforts would help to bring a lasting peace.

Contents

Acknowledgements	ix
Preface	xi
Introduction	1

CHAPTER 1
Acts of leadership and sustainable peace … 9

CHAPTER 2
Collaborative leadership … 29

CHAPTER 3
Transformational leadership … 51

CHAPTER 4
Trauma-informed leadership … 73

CHAPTER 5
Sustainable peace and political leadership … 95

Postscript … 119

Abbreviations and political groups … 123

Political stakeholders (February 2024)   127

Recommended reading   133

Acknowledgements

Thank you to family, friends and colleagues for their encouragement and support.

Thank you to all the people who contributed to insightful and invaluable discussions about post-conflict peacebuilding including: Science and Nonduality, Somatic Experiencing International, The Monroe Institute and the International Body Psychotherapy Journal.

Thank you to Rachel Gristwood at Well Read Proofreading Services for timely feedback and professional guidance. "What a team!"

Thank you to Tony Mason and his colleagues at Peter Lang for making the publication of this book possible.

Preface

A chance conversation with a respected journalist and writer on Northern Ireland gave me the motivation to write about sustainable peace. It was spring 2023, and perfect timing for a new project. Within days, I noticed an opinion piece on Northern Ireland politics from a respected academic which triggered an inexplicable fury within me: I was reading language that incited hatred.

The first experience helped me to clarify my purpose for researching the notion of sustainable peace and meet the requirements for a book proposal. The second experience brought a single-minded energy and passion to research sustainable peace from both theoretical and practical perspectives, and to establish the conditions needed to achieve it.

My choice of Northern Ireland as the context for the book was based on the 2022 General Election when a republican party, Sinn Féin, won and their leader, Michelle O'Neill, became First Minister designate. This election win challenged the political status quo of unionist governments since 1921. It also represented a major political opportunity that opened up for the republican movement. A seismic shift in Northern Ireland's politics had taken place and created an ideal context to take a closer look at the impact that political leaders have on peace processes.

During my research, each new track brought me back to the same place: leadership. I discovered that acts of leadership come in many guises, and they are not always the work of one person. Acts of leadership were observed from the managers of healthcare services, charities, community organisations and members of the public. It became clear that leadership behaviours are different from leadership roles, and this differentiation can be a major issue for people in positions of power and for the people they have been elected to serve. A relationship between leadership behaviours and sustainable peace emerged as a key research outcome which subsequently became a major theme in this book. Sustainable peace is served by leaders who are able to discern when a collaborative approach is more likely to achieve a positive political outcome, and when it is necessary to take a stand.

I have brought lived experience, professional expertise and substantial evidence together in this book, and hope it provides a thoughtful and insightful yet challenging read.

Sally Watson
Lancaster, February 2024

Introduction

Preamble and purpose

The purpose of this book is to explore the political and social conditions needed to secure sustainable peace and the different forms of leadership, all of which support a transition from violent conflict to peace. A practical case study of civil conflict in Northern Ireland and the subsequent peace process will be used to illustrate the critical role that leadership plays in stabilising and transforming a post-conflict society, and in creating the conditions for sustainable peace.

The first three chapters will challenge assumptions on what is meant by leadership and differentiate this from traditional views on the role of leaders. Historical evidence from Northern Ireland's peace process will be used to illustrate the forms of leadership that facilitate conflict transformation, a societal state characterised by a clear political mission and with observable signs of lasting change. In contrast, sustainable peace is defined as a future state with a longer-term vision, which requires new forms of leadership and a new paradigm of political collaboration.

Chapters 4 and 5 will address contemporary social and political challenges in Northern Ireland, the possibility of sustainable peace and the leadership capacity and capability needed to achieve it.

Examples of discourse will be used throughout this book to illustrate the relationship between leadership, language and sustainable peace. In this book, the term discourse applies to spoken language, symbols, rituals and stories, which are used to communicate ideas and interests e.g. warrior discourses include war-like language, symbolic images, heroic stories and marches designed to rally supporters and threaten opponents.

We will journey back in time to understand specific acts of leadership and study the impact they had on conflict resolution, transformation and peacebuilding. As we journey, the past will reveal powerful lessons about the fragility of sustainable peace and provide practical insights for leaders today.

This is not a traditional textbook and the content and style are designed to encourage the reader to use the material to think and feel their way through what leadership means in a contemporary world dominated by war and violent conflicts. For those readers less familiar with the Northern Ireland peace process, there is a glossary of abbreviations with explanatory notes at the back of the book.

1998: "The Troubles" and the peace process

The Northern Ireland peace process was a critical moment in an extended civil conflict that started in the late 1960s. At the time, the Northern Ireland Civil Rights Association (NICRA) was lobbying a Protestant/unionist-led government for greater equality for Catholic citizens. Groups loyal to the union of Northern Ireland and the British crown started to physically attack Catholic communities and specifically NICRA protest marches. The escalation of violence was rapid and within months republican groups had joined the violence, initially to protect a wider Catholic/nationalist community. The Royal Ulster Constabulary (RUC) was caught in the middle and under siege from the scale of community violence. The unionist government formally requested help from the British Prime Minister and British soldiers were sent to Northern Ireland to keep the peace. From 1969 until 1998, the people of Northern Ireland lived with, and were victims of "The Troubles" a euphemistic term for a violent conflict that resulted in over 3,500 deaths, of which 52 % were civilians.

The rapid escalation of civil violence in 1969 has its roots in the partition of Ireland in May 1921 when the British Government divided Ireland into two self-governing entities: Northern Ireland and Southern Ireland. By December 1921, Southern Ireland had become the Irish Free State (now the Irish Republic). The Northern Irish Government chose to remain in the United Kingdom (UK). Since partition, Irish nationalists and republicans have continued to seek a united Ireland while unionists and loyalists wish to remain part of the UK. Today, the politics of partition remain a major challenge, which is further complicated by the religious beliefs of Protestantism and Catholicism.

In 1998, a peace process was initiated by the signing of the Belfast/Good Friday Agreement. The agreement provided a legal basis for future peacebuilding and a clear structure for a power-sharing model of governance in Northern Ireland. Key to initiating peace was the "Principle of Consent" which guaranteed that there would be no change to the sovereignty of Northern Ireland without the consent of a majority.

The agreement acted as a holding pattern between conflicting parties to establish new political structures and start the process of social and political reform. It did not, however, initiate the level of trust or quality of relationships between key stakeholders that would be needed to establish transformational change. From the perspective of a major conflict, the Belfast/Good Friday Agreement was a political success, but for the people of Northern Ireland, the conditions for sustainable peace were not in place:

> Even after the Good Friday Agreement, the unionists and republicans were still unreconciled peoples. With all the history that had gone on before, they simply could not make the leap of faith in the other side.[1]

Fast forward to 2023

> Listening to the Sinn Féin hypocrites made me sick to my stomach. The old IRA and the new are no different. In refusing to acknowledge this truth, Sinn Féin allows republican violence and hatred to fester.[2]

This is an example of clumsy and potentially reckless political discourse from an eminent academic, journalist and unionist supporter. The language is visceral, inflammatory and incites hatred. Consider the tone and content of the following statement made by a senior republican leader in response to intense criticism at her presence at the coronation of a British monarch:

> We live in changing times and it was a respectful thing to do and to be here for all those people at home. I had said that I would be a first minister for all. Attendance here is honouring that and fulfilling my promise.³

This second statement is a carefully crafted example of peace discourse, which reflects a measured tone and inclusive content, and establishes a skilful claim to the moral high ground. Both examples of political discourse are coded messages rather than carriers of absolute truth and provide an insight into two quite different political agendas, forms of leadership and modes of communication. Both statements are valid in the context of Northern Ireland politics, but only one supports sustainable peace.

Warrior discourse and sustainable peace

A characteristic of a post-conflict society is that warrior discourses leak into political speeches, undermining the leadership work of implementing the conditions of a peace treaty. This can be observed through three human phenomena: sacred values, political identities and polarisation.

Sacred values and noble causes

Warrior discourses mobilise people to share a common purpose, follow a specific cause and justify their collective rights to protect that cause. Sacred values are usually associated with a religious cause but they can also extend to social, political and environmental issues.

A key characteristic is passionate rhetoric that encourages followers to transcend self-interest in order to protect and defend a shared "noble" cause.

Political and ethnic identities

The rise of identity politics is a modern global trend fueled by new and old forms of warrior discourses, and the catalytic effect of social media. A clear identity can bring a sense of belonging with others, but a danger lies in the emergence of "them" and "us" labels. Warrior language can transform a workable relationship between individuals and groups into an alarming scale of indirect and direct violence.

Our attachment to an identity is a natural human response but it also plays a significant role in perpetuating conflict. The memories of past grievances, abuses and atrocities become the "noble" causes for other generations to follow.

Warrior discourses and polarisation

Language can simplify a complex political scenario into polarised positions. Terms such as "enemy" and "battle", if taken out of context, can heighten emotional reactions irrespective of the reason or scope of the conflict. The warrior language embedded in sectarian abuse and violence in Northern Ireland reflects an assumption that one group will, over time, dominate the outcome e.g. there will be a united Ireland or a United Kingdom. Today, this form of polarisation continues to trap political leaders into historical positions and impact the quality of leadership and governance. An old paradigm of religious, political and ethnic division cannot be transformed if the political regime is unable to embrace a new paradigm.

"The Troubles" and a new generation

At the time of writing, sectarian violence remains a feature of life in Northern Ireland despite significant progress in peacebuilding and conflict transformation. In the two illustrations below, the first involved a Protestant girl in a shopping centre in a predominantly Catholic area, and the second involved some Catholic friends returning from a football match:

> *3 April 2023*
>
> A 12 year-old girl is set upon by a group, kicked in the head, side and back "for being a Prod".
>
> 6 April 2023
>
> An 18 year-old man wearing a Gaelic sports top is asked his religion. He replies Catholic. He is punched in the face, one friend is savagely kicked and a third is stamped upon.[4]

These young people were not born during "The Troubles", peace talks or subsequent peace building and yet they have inherited, along with their attackers, the traumatic legacy of sectarianism. Incidents of this nature threaten the progress made in conflict transformation and signal that despite the Belfast/Good Friday Agreement, sustainable peace remains an elusive prospect.

Sustainable peace or sustainable conflict?

In the next chapter, we will examine acts of leadership that have sustained efforts in peacemaking and contrast them with acts of leadership that escalated conflict conditions and sustained violence. Conflict resolution and subsequent peace treaties are traditionally conducted by a configuration of military leaders, political leaders and third-party negotiators. This results in a predictable path where political changes to address the root causes of the conflict are generally contingent on an end to violence.

This is a perfectly logical progression towards resolving the conflict, but it also lays the ground for competing agendas, dissent and impasse. This can be observed in the inevitable political battle of wills over ceasefires and humanitarian pauses as the competing warrior language spills over into attempts to secure peace.

A peace treaty is no guarantee of sustainable peace because the forms of leadership needed for conflict resolution are primarily focused on representing conflicting interests rather than on a longer-term mission of conflict transformation.

For now, consider these words from a young refugee who fled from the former Yugoslavia in 1994 and who wrote these words in 2023:

> I wonder how many generations will carry attachment to the pain and hurt we caused each other in that war.[5]

Notes

1. Powell, J. (2009) *Great Hatred, Little Room: Making Peace in Northern Ireland*, London, Vintage Books, pp. 312–313.
2. Dudley Edwards, R. (2023) <https://www.dailymail.co.uk/columnists/article-11786815/Listening-Sinn-Fein-hypocrites-sick-stomach-writes-RUTH-DUDLEY-EDWARDS.html> *Daily Mail*. Accessed 24 August 2023.
3. O'Neill, M. (2023) *Republican News*, 6 May 2023, p. 1.
4. Both incidents, 3 April 2023 and 4 April 2023, were reported in *Irish Republican News* on 6 April 2023.
5. Kuhn, N. (2023) Fragments of War, *International Body Psychotherapy Journal*, 21 (2), 59–69.

CHAPTER 1

Acts of leadership and sustainable peace

Introduction: Acts of leadership

The style and quality of leadership are fundamental factors in the process of building peace and, importantly, sustaining it. The history of "The Troubles" in Northern Ireland reveals acts of leadership that positively affect a wider community of peacemakers as well as the peace process. Some acts of leadership emerged from unexpected places and involved people who were not in positions of power or authority. Not all acts of leadership had a positive outcome and may have incited resistance and escalated violence. Some acts of leadership were missed opportunities, ignored or so discreet that they have only come to light in recent years.

This chapter will establish a relationship between acts of leadership and sustainable peace and set the scene for later chapters. Short case studies will be used to illustrate the different forms of leadership that support conflict resolution and peacebuilding. A conceptual model of leadership approaches will be presented and used to analyse key moments when Northern Ireland pendulated between war and peace.

"Why in God's name?"

On 18 April 2019, Lyra McKee, a journalist, was shot dead by a masked sniper as she observed rioting in Creggan a Catholic area of Derry in Northern Ireland. A few days later, the New IRA released a statement admitting to the crime and describing it as a "mistake". Father Martin

Magill who presided over Lyra's funeral demonstrated a clear act of leadership:

> I commend our political leaders for standing together in Creggan on Good Friday. I am however left with a question: 'Why in God's name does it take the death of a 29-year-old woman with her whole life in front of her to get us to this point?'[1]

The leaders of Northern Ireland's main political parties, the DUP, Sinn Féin, the UUP, the SDLP, the Alliance Party and the Green Party, released a joint statement condemning the killing and describing it as "an attack on all the people of this community, an attack on the peace and democratic processes". The poignant question from Father Magill was a direct challenge to political leaders from Northern Ireland, Ireland and Great Britain. His leadership language was a direct reminder of their collective responsibility to lead the peace process and to serve the interests of the people of Northern Ireland.

Leadership in action

Acts of leadership come in various guises. A *command and control approach* is obvious because power rests with an individual or is vested in a hierarchical structure. This will be felt as a top-down ethos where decisions are cascaded, instructions given, and compliance expected. Command and control styles, also known as authoritarian, are a legacy of war. In some situations, this style is appropriate e.g. in the uniformed services and with first responders. It is a less effective style in settings where collaboration is needed across services or organisations.

A major shift came in the 1960s and 1970s when leadership practice evolved into a more *people-centred* approach. The civil rights movement across the world brought a demand for greater individual freedom and equality. Post-Second World War societies were ready for change and generally less compliant. Today *people-centred leadership* remains popular because it invites people to share their views. In the 1980s *situational leadership* became fashionable because it addressed a practical issue that not all people have the same level of confidence, motivation or capability. A situational approach allows the leader to become more directive with inexperienced people and less directive with capable individuals and their teams. This marked a significant shift away from the command and control approach and redefined the leader's role to one of empowering others. The term empowerment a common term today, has its origins in situational leadership.

In the 1990s a new paradigm of leadership emerged which brought fresh ideas on how to involve people in changes that affected them. Major political changes in Germany (with the fall of the Berlin Wall) and the collapse of the Apartheid regime in South Africa challenged the power dynamic between political leaders and civil societies. A successful leader was now seen as competent at facilitating change rather than giving orders. *Transitional leadership* emerged as more appropriate to a smaller scale change with planned steps towards a clearly defined goal. Transitional leadership continues to be popular because the outcomes can be measured, audited and used as evidence that the change has been successful. *Transformational leadership* also emerged in the 1990s in response to the challenges of large-scale political or social change where diverse stakeholders made outcomes unpredictable and rarely stable. Transformational leaders are visionary, charismatic and able to influence people to see the "bigger picture".

Major political and social changes are not always predictable with planned transitions or exciting transformations. Today many of the challenges facing societies across the world require new approaches to change that are more collaborative. In a complex change involving communities, societies and nations a transformational leader can provide a powerful vision and momentum for change but may not be strong enough to influence other leaders to collaborate. An act of transformational leadership can be seen in the energy that Tony Blair, the British Prime Minister, brought to the Belfast/Good Friday Agreement in 1998. His style brought political leaders together to make a peace agreement and create power-sharing structures but he was not able to facilitate the conditions for sustainable peace.

A collaborative leadership approach is more likely to bring consistency and stability after a major change. Collaborative political leaders have the ability to convene and sustain relationships which work for the best interests of the people they serve. They have the courage to persuade other leaders to put their political self-interests to one side. This is a challenging form of leadership for politicians because it involves sharing power.

Community collaboration

On 10 August 1976, a chase involving members of the IRA and British troops took place in West Belfast. Soldiers in a Land Rover were following a car driven by a young republican with a passenger on board. The driver was shot dead and his passenger took the wheel, swerved the car and crashed into a family group. Four children died that day. A significant act of leadership emerged from this tragedy in the creation of a community group called the Peace People. At the time it represented a powerful example of cross-community collaboration for the common cause of peace irrespective of religious, ethnic or political divisions. Below is a clear illustration of the power of leadership and language to influence others to change:

> To blame either the republicans who initiated the chain of incidents resulting in the deaths, or the soldiers who had shot Danny Lennon as he drove through a heavily populated area in broad daylight, seemed almost profane: the core reaction of the community was one of pure anguish at the needless deaths.[2]

In the 1970s the Peace People organisation gained significant support from across Protestant and Catholic communities and has continued to work for peace to the present day. The founders, Máiread Corrigan and Betty Williams, were awarded the Nobel Peace Prize in 1976. Ironically their political success in uniting communities and empowering people was met with opposition and intimidation from both loyalists and republicans. There is an important lesson for sustainable peace from the

Peace People and many of the later charities formed in Northern Ireland. It is clear that grassroots organisations have an important role to play because they have practical leadership experience of collaboration.

A British prime minister takes a risk

A transformational act of leadership worth examining is the role British Prime Minister, Harold Wilson, played in sanctioning backchannel activity in the 1970s. He came to power in 1974 and as leader of the opposition had already met the IRA secretly in Dublin in 1972. An early backchannel between the British Government and republicans had been established to work on the possibility of peace. Much of the communication was not in the public domain but occasionally a coded message would appear from republican leaders. The quotation below reflects a moment in time when the possibility of peace was signalled to the backchannel:

> We want a situation to come about where political advance can take the place of guerilla war. What we see is an honorable accommodation with the British coupled with an honourable accommodation with the loyalists.[3]

During 1973 the backchannel discussed a 10-point plan which included an indefinite republican ceasefire and a series of measures to ensure it was permanent. Two surprises come out of these events: a truce was brokered between the IRA and the British Government, and republican leaders were open to peace through political means. At the time Harold Wilson was discreetly looking to include a consent principle as a way to resolve republican grievances and keep unionist politicians on board. His formula for peace became the Sunningdale Agreement in 1973 and an early attempt by the British Government to find a peaceful solution.

We now know that this early backchannel took significant acts of transformational leadership and individual courage from all the parties involved. The unionist response to Harold Wilson's reforms was to call a general strike and bring chaos to Northern Ireland. As John Hume, a nationalist politician, pointed out an opportunity for peace was lost:

> I've no doubt at all that had the British Government at the time stood firm against the Loyalist Workers' Strike, the Sunningdale Agreement would have stood firm and we would be in a much better position today.[4]

The moment was lost because unionists and their politicians were not involved in the talks. The Sunningdale Agreement represented their worst nightmare and they reacted with loyalist support to protect the union. A major transformational change cannot be stable when some stakeholders are left out in the cold. The same logic applies to sustainable peace.

Men of peace: collaborative acts of leadership

In 1998 David Trimble (UUP) and John Hume (SDLP) were jointly awarded the Nobel Peace Prize. This marked an impressive act of collaborative leadership between two politicians with opposing views on the future of Northern Ireland. The relationship between the two men was characterised by respect and a shared purpose that peace in Northern Ireland was a core priority. Both political leaders demonstrated significant personal courage, especially knowing that their names were on both loyalist and republican paramilitary assassination lists.

In 2023, during a 25-year commemoration of the Belfast/Good Friday Agreement, their sons were asked what their fathers would have thought of the current impasse between politicians. Their responses illustrate how transformational and collaborative leaders see the world:

> Dad would try and think his way out of a problem first (Nicholas Trimble).
>
> He would be doing his damnedest to bring the two sides together, concentrate on the common interest and using that common ground to find a way forward (John Hume, Jr.).[5]

There are legions of courageous people and groups who have worked tirelessly for peace in Northern Ireland, and their actions illustrate how important the quality and style of leadership are to sustainable peace. Acts of transformational and collaborative leadership are happening all the time across Northern Ireland and they need to be acknowledged, learned from and supported.

The journey to sustainable peace

Any discussion of sustainable peace in Northern Ireland needs to factor in the wise counsel of Johan Galtung, a pioneer in the discipline of peace studies, who introduced the terms *positive* and *negative peace*.[6] His work brought an entirely different perspective to conflict resolution. A decision to end direct violence through a ceasefire is negative peace and unlikely to morph immediately into sustainable peace. For positive peace, the root causes of conflict need to be addressed and a systemic approach agreed to initiate reform. Galtung regarded sustainable peace as an achievable goal if peacebuilding structures were created in parallel with the development of community capacity for peace management and conflict resolution. In practice, this does not mean top-down political leadership or bottom-up community engagement but an integrated strategy developed collaboratively and with adequate funding. A whole system change requires leadership at all levels focused on a powerful vision, clear strategy and collaborative working relationships. If we apply these ideas to sustainable peace in Northern Ireland, then a whole system approach has not been achieved. The political leaders of the Northern Ireland Executive do not share power in a collaborative sense.

The structural reforms written into the Belfast/Good Friday Agreement in 1998 were based on the principle of inclusivity e.g. power-sharing bodies, human rights legislation, and the consent principle and decommissioning. It was a compromise that did not have full support from paramilitary republican and loyalist groups or indeed some political supporters of unionism and republicanism.

A hallmark of the Belfast/Good Friday Agreement was the scale of effort put into formal negotiations and the drumbeat of deadlines. Tony Blair, the new Prime Minister, was keen to score an early political goal by brokering peace in Northern Ireland. He brought a high-energy transformational leadership approach to initiate conflict resolution. There was a strong emphasis on getting to agreement but less weight given to trust building and developing quality relationships. The participating politicians negotiated the terms of an agreement but there is little evidence that they felt a sense of collective responsibility for leading the province into peace. An enlightening remark from the chief negotiator, Jonathan Powell, illustrates a major barrier to sustainable peace in Northern Ireland:

> Crucially, attempts at conflict resolution will only succeed where both sides come to realise they cannot win. In Northern Ireland, the two traditions still do not agree.[7]

Sustainable peace and polarised communities

At the time of writing, a clear example of religious and cultural polarisation can be observed in the annual ritual of eleventh night bonfires. The bonfires mark a military victory for a Protestant King, William of Orange, over a Catholic King, James II. The date was 1690. The historical ritual of bonfires has involved more menace than an annual celebration because it includes the burning of nationalist flags, images and effigies. As Gary McCleave, Sinn Féin MP, wrote in 2022:

> I have to answer questions from my children, who came across the image on social media, why their daddy is on a bonfire to be burnt.[8]

Despite the achievements of the Belfast/Good Friday Agreement, the rituals of loyalist bonfires and republican Easter Rising commemorations reflect the entrenched positions over religious legacies and different political views on the sovereignty of Northern Ireland. The warrior language embedded in these rituals acts as a powerful barrier to sustainable peace. Language provides labels to cluster people into Protestants, unionists and loyalists on one hand and Catholics, nationalists and republicans on the other. The result is political shorthand which continues to shape a society of diverse and multiple identities into two traditional groupings.

There are religious differences between Catholics and Protestants on how, as mortals, we relate to God. Catholicism has church teachings and intermediaries such as priests and saints to help guide people in their Christian faith. Protestantism relies on the Bible as God's word and a primary source of knowledge on how to live a Christian life. Both theologies offer powerful and sacred instructions on the practice of forgiveness and the power of peace. Despite precise differences on the ways to access God, both belief systems share common ground in their Christianity.

When religious beliefs become entangled with political and ethnic identities, the polarising effect of religion magnifies difference. John Hume's words in 1964 were a profound message for political leaders at the time. His words have even greater significance for sustainable peace:

> One of the greatest contributions a Catholic in Northern Ireland can make to a liberalising of the political atmosphere would be the removal of the equation between Nationalist and Catholic.[9]

In the present day, there are positive signs of change, especially in the middle ground of politics, with the Alliance and Green Parties growing their share of the vote to add to that of the SDLP and the UUP. In a middle ground, new relationships and collaborations are possible which can steadily influence social and political change. This is also demonstrated with a greater integration of Protestant and Catholic schools and marriages. However, it is clear that sustainable peace will require further collaboration across traditional political divisions and a gradual uncoupling of religious values from political identities.

Acts of leadership and "The Troubles"

A picture is starting to emerge from the forms of leadership that contribute to peacebuilding. The spectrum of command and control to transformational and collaborative styles provides an understanding of the choices a leader has in any given situation. Each of the forms of leadership discussed earlier in this chapter represents a legitimate response, but their impact may have had unexpected, unpredicted and dangerous consequences. In the 1970s, several acts of leadership contributed to the escalation of violence. Unionist political leaders in Stormont and British politicians largely opted for a "command and control" approach and then found it impossible to negotiate for peace. At the time, advocates for peace in both governments were known as "wets".

A spontaneous combustion of events in Northern Ireland created the conditions for civil unrest which were quickly followed by sectarian violence. A civil rights movement had been lobbying the unionist-led government for greater equality for Catholics since 1968. The chain of events that followed was fast and furious. Loyalist groups demonstrated their support for unionism and the British crown by attacking Catholic communities. Republicans responded by defending with force, both by Catholics and the wider nationalist community. The Royal Ulster Constabulary (RUC) attempted to bring law and order and British soldiers joined in the chaos as peacekeepers.

An escalation of violence on this scale and speed is characteristic of unplanned and uncoordinated command and control. Political and military leaders generally respond to a crisis by taking control and setting in motion protocols for action. The need for a rapid response can draw them into behaving tactically to get results. In the early days of "The Troubles" the tactics employed by politicians and security services now appear to have been grounded in brute force with a mission to restore order. At best, this was an exercise in negative peace, but the outcomes simply fanned the flames of violence.

Civil rights movement

August 1969 was a pivotal month in Northern Ireland shaped by an explosive combination of civil rights activity and overzealous policing. Both John Hume and Bernadette Devlin were civil rights activists and had pivotal roles working for greater justice, fairness and equality for Catholic communities. In Derry/Londonderry, planned peaceful civil rights marches were met with loyalist violence and law enforcement led by the RUC. In April 1969, at the age of 21, Bernadette Devlin had won a seat in the House of Common as an independent republican. John Hume became the founder of SDLP and a significant contributor to the peace process.

The Northern Ireland Civil Rights Association (NICRA) was a major embarrassment to the unionist-led government because it highlighted the scale of disenfranchisement of Catholics. On the ground Ian Paisley (DUP) voiced a deeply ingrained unionist fear of social and political reform in Northern Ireland. His language "They breed like rabbits and multiply like vermin" was instrumental in loyalist rampages into Catholic communities. As both a religious and political leader, he had the power to change attitudes and influence a peaceful outcome.

In the early 1970s, the IRA found themselves unprepared for the scale of loyalist violence in Belfast and Londonderry/Derry. Trust in the impartiality of the RUC evaporated quickly and, to the dismay of the Northern Ireland Government, the police lost control. The RUC and their predecessors, the B specials, were viewed by Catholics as loyalist thugs. In terms of political leadership, in a short time period unionist politicians had lost control of their own government and public order. An opportunity to address legitimate concerns for greater freedom, equality and justice was lost. In the eyes of nationalist communities, the unionist government had reneged on a duty of care for their safety.

British military leadership (August 1969)

In August 1969 British troops were deployed on the streets of Northern Ireland under a legal provision known as Military Aid to the Civil Power (MACP) following a request from the unionist government. In theory the mission was to keep the peace and support the RUC. In practice, it went badly wrong and made matters worse.

A peacekeeping mission is not an exercise in sustainable peace but a crisis intervention to prevent further violence. The military units who arrived had some training in peacekeeping but not specifically in urban techniques e.g. civilian stop and search. MACP has a very different remit to MACC (Military Aid to the Civil Community) whose soldiers drive ambulances and help with floods. MACP is a very serious decision for a government to make because it destabilises the relationship between the state and the people. In Northern Ireland British soldiers were being used to police communities of British citizens.

Bloody Sunday, Derry/Londonderry

Bloody Sunday, 30 January 1972, was a military disaster because it illustrated the fine line between engaging in conflict prevention and getting drawn into the politics of the conflict. On the day soldiers went beyond their mission to keep the peace and responded to what they believed was ahead of them i.e. battlefield conditions. The first shots were from British soldiers with live ammunition. There were 13 civilian deaths at a civil rights march, and decades later, Lord Saville's report concluded that there was no evidence of shots fired by republican snipers. The first shot fired was from a British paratrooper.[10] A closer examination of the language used by the military commander to brief his soldiers reveals a scene set for a bloody fight:

> In my view this was a war. When we moved on streets, we moved as if we were moving against a well-armed, well-trained army. I wanted my soldiers to stay alive and I actually said to them, 'You will not get killed'.[11]

British soldiers, generally, do not go to war for a political cause. They follow orders, their instincts and look out for each other. At the first shot/death, soldiers will regroup and use their training and instincts to survive. Their survival responses are both primal and automatic, training and team spirit. On the 30 January 1972, the first death was a civilian, and the event was not a battle. The political decisions to deploy soldiers, the choice of regiment and the military leadership on Bloody Sunday were seriously flawed.

Republicans already had their noble cause of a united Ireland and the IRA now had reason to prepare for guerilla warfare. From a republican perspective, a unionist government supported by the British state continued to deny them their human rights. The fight for a united Ireland was a galvanising mission and although republican leaders realised it could be a "Long War", recruitment into the IRA during the early 1970s was at an all-time high.

The notion of a war with the British state took a firm grip on the republican psyche and their warrior language drew on the Easter Rising, 1916, as a way to legitimise the armed struggle against the British Army. IRA violence over much of the next decade drowned out the legitimate political goals of nationalists seeking greater equality and opportunity:

> The Irish republic was proclaimed by the only way possible, by force of arms and only by force of arms can the Republic we seek be established.[12]

Internment and criminalisation

On 9 August 1971, 3,000 British troops carried out a pre-emptive strike and raided republican/nationalist communities to arrest republican leaders. Of the 342 arrests that morning, there were no loyalists despite evidence of their involvement in sectarian attacks. It was an ill-conceived plan, which was ironically a collaborative effort between the unionist-led Northern Ireland Government, the RUC and the British Army. Hundreds of young Catholic men were imprisoned without trial and the Special Powers Act used to interrogate them. Republicans already had a powerful sacred cause, internment simply confirmed that a brutal political regime existed in Northern Ireland, aided and abetted by the RUC and the British security system. Prison became another battlefront for IRA volunteers.

In terms of military leadership, the involvement of soldiers in Bloody Sunday and the internments was a disaster because it radicalised another generation of republicans and brought reputational damage to the British Army. The decision to deploy the Parachute Regiment as a peacekeeping force into Derry/Londonderry was a blunt instrument and a contributing factor in turning Northern Ireland into a war zone. British soldiers were put in an impossible position and found themselves part of the collateral damage that occurs when political and military leaders make decisions which fail to consider the long impact on civilian communities. The involvement of soldiers in Northern Ireland and the subsequent treatment of republican prisoners turned them into noble warriors with new forms of warrior talk to account for IRA operations:

> Evidence confronts us of the determination of the British Government to pursue its senseless policy of military oppression. The Irish Republican Army has no choice but to continue the campaign of armed resistance.[13]

The Sunningdale Agreement in 1973 had included an assurance that republican prisoners would be treated as prisoners of war and given special category status. It was not honoured and special category status became a flashpoint that led to the republican hunger strikes in 1981–1982. The status of IRA prisoners is a really important issue for republicans and one which predates the events of 1969. The partition of Ireland in 1920 is seen as an illegal act and republicans argue that their prisoners of war are not terrorists or criminals but freedom fighters.

Meanwhile, senior British Army officers who had learned their craft from previous wars and conflict zones across the world devised British military strategies in Northern Ireland over the next decade. They were not natural peacemakers. The stage was set for an escalation in hostilities. In the 1980s, senior military leaders became increasingly aware of the flaws in the British Government's analysis of republicanism and had the courage to voice it:

> Peace can only reign when there is a political solution and the military situation is contained. The IRA will never be totally defeated. The cause of republicanism will remain as long as Ireland is divided.[14]

Throughout the 1970s and 1980s the political agenda of unionist leaders continued to dominate the British Government's policy towards Northern Ireland. Republicans continued to wage their "noble war" and loyalists, true to their mantra of "no surrender", fought back with a vengeance. British soldiers settled down for multiple tours in Northern Ireland with no further pretence that they were keeping the peace. Between the start of "The Troubles" in 1969 and the final phase of decommissioning in 2007, 1441 military personnel died as a result of operations in Northern Ireland. In the same period of time, the British military killed 301 people of whom 50 % were civilians.[15]

Paramilitary leadership

In addition to the presence of British soldiers in the 1970s, Northern Ireland was gridlocked with paramilitary organisations. The IRA Army Council was in control of republican military operations with Sinn Féin operating as their political wing. Loyalist paramilitary groups were many and diverse in nature with a mission to defend the sovereignty of Northern Ireland. All paramilitary groups had command structures and military ranks with varying degrees of internal discipline.

By 1977 the IRA leadership had revised their "Green Book", a manual for all republican volunteers with detailed guidance on training, behaviour and discipline. Their command and control form of leadership and organisation was ironically similar to the British Army's. The Green Book revisions included guerilla warfare tactics and a reorganisation into a dispersed cell structure.

At the same time, loyalist paramilitaries operated as two main groups, the Ulster Freedom Fighters (UFF) and the Ulster Defence Association (UDA). The relationship with violence of these loyalist groups is clear from their choice of name, and borne of intense fear of Northern Ireland being absorbed into the republic of Ireland. Loyalist groups were more diverse and disparate in the way they operated and this pattern has continued to the present day. Both loyalist and republican paramilitaries have experienced internal conflicts with volunteers leaving to start new groups or join existing splinter groups.

By 1979, the conditions for peace in any form, negative, positive or sustainable, were in practical terms non-existent. A population of just over 1.5 million was living in a war zone. This was when Margaret Thatcher became the British Prime Minister.

Leadership and the "Iron Lady"

The precise status of republican prisoners became a long running issue for the British Government. The special category status had been rescinded on 1 March 1976, which meant republicans engaged in armed struggle were categorised as criminals. In protest, republican prisoners refused to wear a prison uniform and started a "blanket protest" and used a prison blanket as their only form of clothing. This escalated into a "dirty protest" where republican prisoners refused to bathe, use a lavatory or clean their cells. The British Government continued to refuse to grant special category status and the shocking sanitary conditions brought international attention to the degradation and dehumanisation of republican prisoners. British political leaders reasoned that republicans had brought the appalling prison conditions on themselves and failed to realise the implications of creating more republican martyrs. It proved to be a command and control approach that misread the scale and potency of the republican sacred cause to reunite Ireland.

Below is an extract of a statement by republican prisoners on 1 March 1981, and a predictable response to the command and control leadership demonstrated by the British Government and its security services at the time:

> We are political prisoners and everything about our arrests, interrogations, trials and prison conditions show we are politically motivated and not motivated by selfish reasons for selfish ends. As further demonstration of the justice of our cause, a number of our comrades, beginning today with Bobby Sands, will hunger strike to the death.[16]

Special category status acknowledged that republicans were prisoners of war and this was important to the republican psyche because it brought dignity and legitimisation to their historic struggle. During the 1970s, internment and criminalisation strategies, the brainchild of unionist leaders and the British Government, filled prisons with republicans. When Margaret Thatcher became Prime Minister in 1979, she made it clear that she was not negotiating with republican "terrorists". A female warrior had arrived with a remarkable lack of understanding of Northern Ireland politics or Irish republicanism.

Hunger striking became another battlefront for republican volunteers in prison. The purpose of hunger strikes was to bring attention to republican suffering, conduct a dignified rebellion and shame the British Government in the eyes of the world. It seemed a lost cause but the knowledge that ten young men had volunteered for a slow agonising death rallied massive political support across nationalist communities.

In 1981, Bobby Sands, the first hunger striker to die, was already an elected republican MP with the right to a seat in the British Parliament. It was a powerful indicator of electoral support from both nationalists and republicans and the beginning of a political transformation for Sinn Féin. In total, 10 republican hunger strikers died in 1981. Another generation of martyrs had made their contribution to the sacred cause of republicanism:

> What compels young men to die?
> A death so long and cruel
> To suffer years of pain and shame
> In solitary, in jails?[17]

Margaret Thatcher's leadership during the hunger strikes brought short-term notoriety and accolades from supporters but her command and control approach brought unexpected consequences for Sinn Féin leaders and set them on a major political transformation and entry into mainstream politics. The election of Bobby Sands opened up the possibility that the republican movement could take a political route towards a united Ireland. The subsequent political transformation of Sinn Féin as a political party and their contribution to the peace process will be outlined in the next chapter.

Whether Margaret Thatcher appreciated the longer-term political consequences of her leadership style is difficult to assess from her warrior discourse:

> Mr. Sands was a convicted criminal who chose to take his own life.[18]

> Faced with the failure of their discredited campaign, the men of violence have chosen in recent months to play what may be their last card.[19]

Republicans had not played their last card. Between 1980 and 1981 an existing backchannel between the IRA and the British Government was active. The British side of the backchannel did not want any more republican deaths and IRA leaders were open to compromise. The republican hunger strikes were initially not sanctioned by the IRA Army Council who feared that a new prison "battlefront" would prove a distraction from military operations in Northern Ireland and on the British mainland. Republican prisoners wanted to "do their bit" and under the leadership of Bobby Sands made a stand. Their martyrdom not only radicalised another generation of young people, it also opened up the possibility of a political route to Irish unity:

> We believe that an age-old struggle for Irish self-determination has been immeasurably advanced by this hunger strike and therefore we claim a massive political victory.[20]

The leadership cards played by Margaret Thatcher and her government set the cause of peace back for another decade. For the rest of the 1980s backchannel activity was minimal but there were several acts of collaborative leadership in the form of discreet conversations about peace e.g. Hume-Adams talks and informal discussions between the British and Irish Governments.

Chapter summary

A transformational change in society is mobilised by forms of leadership that facilitate human interaction e.g. person-centred, situational, transformational and collaborative. To illustrate this, a continuum of forms of leadership has been presented with practical examples. These range from traditional command and control leadership to collaborative approaches that align more closely with the speed of change in modern society. All forms of leadership on the continuum are valid, but the manner in which political leaders communicate can have a significant impact on whether the conflict will be resolved or escalated.

The chapter has demonstrated that specific acts of leadership from individuals or groups across several decades demonstrate the capability and resourcefulness of the people of Northern Ireland to build sustainable peace. Sustainable peace in Northern Ireland is not insurmountable, but it requires a major transformation in the way politicians engage with each other and make leadership decisions. Collaboration is at the heart of sustainable peace and this is a tough challenge for the current political regime, which remains dominated by issues of sovereignty rather than addressing the priorities of social change and transformation.

Notes

1. *Irish Times,* 24 April 2019, p. 1.
2. www.peacepeople Peace People, the Beginnings, p. 1.
3. *Republican News*, April 1974.
4. Hume, J. quoted in Drover, G. (1995) *John Hume: Man of Peace*, London: Vista, 1995, p. 70.
5. O'Carroll, L. (2023) "Trimble and Hume's sons say fathers would have broken the Stormont deadlock", *The Guardian*, 7 April 2023, p. 1.
6. Galtung, J. (1996) *Peace by Peaceful Means: Peace and Conflict, Development and Civilization*, London, Sage Publications. He is known as the "father of peace studies".

7. Powell, J. (2008) Great *Hatred, Little Room*, Vintage Books, London, p. 321.
8. McCleave, G. *Republican News*, 11 July 2022.
9. Hume, J. (1964) The Northern Catholic, *The Irish Times*, 18–19 May, p. 1.
10. Report of the Bloody Sunday Inquiry, <https://www.gov.uk/government/publications/report-of-the-bloody-sunday-inquiry>, 15 June 2010.
11. Taylor, P. (1997) *Provos: The IRA and Sinn Féin*, London, Bloomsbury, pp. 114–115.
12. *An Phoblacht*, April 1970, p. 1.
13. *An Phoblacht*, 30 March 1973, p. 1.
14. General Sir James Glover quoted in Taylor, P. (2023) *Operation Chiffon: The Secret Story of MI5 and MI6 and the Road to Peace in Ireland*, London, Bloomsbury Publishing, p. 127.
15. Mills, C. and Torrance, D. (2022) Investigation of former Armed Forces personnel who served in Northern Ireland, *House of Commons Library*, 18 May 2022.
16. O'Rawe, R. (2005) *Blanketmen: The untold story of the H-Block hunger strike, Dublin*: New Island, p. 123.
17. Hurson, M. (2023) A poem written by a republican hunger striker, *Irish Republican News*, 13 July 2023, p. 8.
18. Taylor, P. (1992) BBC interview with Colonel Derek Wilford, Commanding Officer, Parachute Regiment, cited in Taylor, P. (1997) Provos*: The IRA and Sinn Féin*, London, Bloomsbury, p. 114.
19. Margaret Thatcher's speech to the House of Commons, 5 May 1981, <https://www.margaretthatcher.org/document/>.
20. *An Phoblacht*, 10 October 1981.

CHAPTER 2

Collaborative leadership

Reflections and insights

Chapter 1 provided examples of transformational and collaborative leaders who had the vision to see a bigger picture for Northern Ireland beyond sectarian division. Some of these leaders worked discreetly and in backchannels; others developed practical proposals to address the root causes of conflict. There were examples of people with minimal power to bring about change who, through courage and with good hearts, made a significant difference.

In Northern Ireland a major challenge to sustainable peace lies with political leaders; specifically the Executive and their willingness to share power for a long enough period of time to learn how to govern wisely. The Belfast/Good Friday Agreement in 1998 was a historic peace agreement, which addressed power sharing, promised an end to violence and made provisions for social, economic and political reforms necessary. This chapter will examine the agreement from the perspective of leadership, negotiating processes, backchannel activities and the unfinished peacebuilding and political work that faces political leaders today:

> To achieve these lofty ideals, devolved government would have to make a difference to people's everyday lives and relationships. Saying it was one thing, but delivering on the grand rhetoric would prove to be much more difficult.[1]

How peace was brokered

> If the Good Friday Agreement endures, it will be because it is fair and balanced. It is based on the principle that the future of Northern Ireland should be decided by the people of Northern Ireland, and it seeks to promote tolerance and mutual respect.[2]

The Belfast/Good Friday Agreement was a historic achievement because it forced old enemies to negotiating tables and into the spotlight of international interest. It raised the stakes for the leaders of all political parties but not necessarily their game. It was, however, a testimony to the leadership skill of US Senator George Mitchell in managing the dynamics between diverse political agendas and two governments: British and Irish. An experienced chair, he insisted on clear ground rules and protocols for meetings and confidentiality. This backfired a little in the early months when unionist politicians objected to both his appointment and his ground rules. George Mitchell resisted the temptation to adopt a command and control approach and followed advice from David Trimble, leader of the UUP, to invite the participants to work on their own ground rules. This advice probably saved an early collapse of talks but resulted in months of wrangling about how to conduct the talks:

> My ability to be effective would depend more on my gaining the participant's trust and confidence than on the formal description of my authority.[3]

The "Mitchell Principles" provided clear prerequisites for entry into talks including the cessation of all violence. This proved a big challenge for both republican and loyalist paramilitaries. In the public's perception, Sinn Féin and the IRA were one and the same i.e. "terrorists". At the time, unionist politicians were more skilful at sidestepping the issue of their influence with loyalist paramilitaries.

In 1998, the key to bringing a positive peace was the establishment of new power-sharing structures and transparent governance. The final agreement enshrined the principle of consent to any change in the sovereignty of

Northern Ireland. The consent principle was a signal to unionists that the union was safe in the near future. For republicans, their vision of a united Ireland had been acknowledged and their political aims legitimised. In theory, the political space for an end to violence was created but it took another nine years for both sides to fulfil the terms of the agreement on decommissioning. The consent principle was a vehicle to create "common ground" and a basis for positive peace but it did not guarantee a societal transformation in Northern Ireland or an end to violence.

A low level of trust between unionist and republican politicians remained despite George Mitchell's best efforts. The DUP boycotted talks and refused to sign the final agreement. It is important to acknowledge that for some republican and unionist supporters, the Belfast/Good Friday Agreement represented a shocking compromise. In the aftermath of the final agreement, the conditions for decommissioning were met with a backlash from both loyalist and republican paramilitaries. The complex nature of the objections to decommissioning revealed a fundamentally different relationship with violence:

> Tony Blair said decommissioning was a symbol. He's more right than he can know. To unionists, decommissioning is a symbol of victory over the IRA; to republicans, decommissioning is sign of surrender.[4]

Despite a historic peace agreement, the scene was set for both unresolved political differences and ongoing sectarian violence.

Leadership and the "Chuckle brothers"

In 2007, power sharing became a reality when Ian Paisley, a unionist MP, became First Minister and Martin McGuinness, a republican MP, became deputy First Minister. Two old enemies took office together on 8 May and their speeches conveyed a genuine desire for a workable relationship:

> From the depths of my heart I can say to you today that I believe Northern Ireland has come to a time of peace, a time when hate will no longer rule.[5] (Ian Paisley, senior)

> I want to wish you all the very best as we step forward towards the greatest yet most exciting challenge of our lives. The Office of the First and deputy First Ministers is a good place to start.[6] (Martin McGuinness)

The two extracts reflect a coordinated act of collaborative leadership and an interesting use of peace discourse. If we take a closer look at the encoded deeper messages, there are insights into the challenges the two men were facing from their own supporters. Ian Paisley reminded a national and international audience that Northern Ireland still existed. Martin McGuinness touched on the future implications of power sharing without bringing up Irish unity. Their speeches signalled political unity but the subtle messages were directed internally at their supporters.

The two men walked a tightrope together and came under extreme pressure for appearing to enjoy each other's company. Ian Paisley stepped down in 2008. He was admonished by his own party members for "too much chuckling" in public. Both men took great risks and found a way to lead together despite the early warning signs that the Belfast/Good Friday Agreement had not reached the hearts and minds of all political stakeholders.

In 2014, Martin McGuinness made an address at Ian Paisley's funeral and his words sum up how crucial political collaboration is to sustaining peace:

> Our relationship confounded many. Of course, our political differences continued; his allegiances were to Britain and mine to Ireland. But we were able to work effectively together in the interests of all our people.[7]

Sustainable peace requires political leadership that is based on a shared vision, clear purpose and a collaborative language. In the short lifespan of the Northern Ireland Executive, party political interests and deep-rooted fears have tended to drive out the quality of leadership and collaborative working needed for sustainable peace.

Power-sharing and collaborative leadership

Martin McGuinness remained deputy First Minister until 2017, working with several DUP First Ministers after Ian Paisley. The precision in his speeches demonstrated political wisdom and consistent messages about peace:

> There is hurt on all sides and all of us have a responsibility to recognise that, if we are to consolidate peace and build genuine reconciliation. People like myself, Arlene Foster and all politicians have a role to play by giving positive leadership in the work of reconciliation and coming to terms with the past.[8]

In 2017, Martin McGuinness resigned and the Executive collapsed. The subsequent direct rule from Westminster remained until 2020 and precious time was lost for political leaders to focus on strategic matters. The model of power sharing agreed in 1998 was a system known as *mandatory coalition* as opposed to *voluntary coalition* within which parties negotiate an agreement to share power. The two largest parties are allocated the First Minister and deputy First Minister positions and if one resigns, the other has to follow and the executive collapses. Direct rule from the British Government immediately restricts the devolved government in their financial decision making powers. Westminster takes over health, justice and education and operates through civil servants. This means controversial legislation and budget bills, which affect Northern Ireland, are passed by a British parliament. Political leaders in Northern Ireland have consistently squandered the opportunity to work on meaningful legislation and more importantly to learn how to make power-sharing work.

Since 1999, there has been direct rule in 2000, 2002–2007 and 2017–2020. The power-sharing model was designed to bring "parity of esteem" between the two main identities in Northern Ireland. The frequency of collapses in the Executive since the Paisley/McGuinness partnership indicates that structural change such as power sharing is only one aspect of sustainable peace. In 1998 political leaders had a remarkable opportunity to sustain peace by finding ways to conduct political work strategically, wisely and responsively. In 2008, republican and unionist critics of the "Chuckle brothers" dragged the Executive back to an old world order of division, fear and sectarianism.

The Belfast/Good Friday Agreement in 1998 may have produced the means to address the root causes of conflict but legislation cannot heal wounds, abate fear or silence hatred. The history and culture of the Executive, since 1999 has not been conducive to their development as political leaders. Each round of power sharing, collapse and direct rule has brought political consequences for the Executive and reputational damage to them both individually and collectively. Today, in full view of the world, elected representatives are using the power and authority gifted to them by the electorate to block political opponents, and play barely disguised games:

> They have continued to seek out and cultivate areas of disagreement because disagreeing with each other is what they exist to do.[9]

Constructive ambiguity and unfinished business

A peace process is not a single event as witnessed in high profile signing events between politicians and world leaders. The symbolic exchange of signatures is an important ritual, but it does not guarantee the scale of trust and collaboration required between political leaders to reach an agreement and deliver on the conditions for peace.

It is important for all parties to understand not only the causes of the conflict but to appreciate how the parties involved view the peace process. There is significant emotional work in a peace process especially around the detail and manner of ceasefires and decommissioning of weapons. George Mitchell may have hoped for constructive relationships, but his appointment was resisted and participants got bogged down in procedural detail rather than starting work on substantive issues. Early attempts to collapse the peace talks were circumvented and in the final weeks, the pace ramped up with a series of deadlines to force agreement and bring closure. In the race to the finish "constructive ambiguity" became the approach to get all parties to agree on a binding consent principle, new structures of governance and a process for decommissioning.

A major flaw was the assumption that political leaders engaged in negotiations had the capability and readiness to manage the scale of change needed to bring a sustainable peace. "Constructive ambiguity" brought a positive outcome and structures to build a peaceful peace, but it did not create the conditions to heal a divided society or to encourage new forms of leadership, which would be needed to implement the agreement.

The Belfast/Good Friday Agreement was not the first formal attempt at negotiating peace since the start of "The Troubles" in 1969. Precursors included the Sunningdale Agreement in 1973, the Anglo-Irish Agreement in 1986 and the Downing Street Declaration in 1993. The approach and aftermath of these agreements illustrate that conflict resolution is not a one-off process but may move through different phases. Movement through phases is not necessarily linear or predictable, especially if there is unfinished political business or a delayed disarmament. Different stages of conflict resolution are provided below with some practical examples that illustrate why it is imperative that political leaders have a comprehensive understanding of the complexity and dynamics of conflicts.

Conflict prevention involves action to de-escalate violence. It encompasses third-party mediation, formal emergency talks, discreet backchannel explorations and military intervention. In 1969, the British Government opted for a military intervention and British soldiers were mobilised to police communities caught up in sectarian violence. Military intervention was deemed to be an expedient strategy but it had the opposite effect and escalated the violence. This made it very difficult for all stakeholders to pull back and engage in other options to stabilise Northern Ireland. This was not a well-planned conflict prevention strategy but a calamitous chain of events that trapped the citizens of Northern Ireland into decades of violent conflict

Conflict settlement involves negotiations to end violence and start a peace process. The Sunningdale Agreement in 1973 was a British Government proposal to create a power-sharing executive, a cross-border

Council of Ireland and start the process of social and economic reforms. It was formulated on the basis of backchannel discussions between the British Government and the IRA. Unionist politicians were incandescent and saw it as evidence that a united Ireland was being planned behind their backs. The combined force of unionist power and loyalist violence stopped the agreement in its tracks. The Sunningdale Agreement guaranteed the principle of consent.

The Anglo-Irish Agreement (1985) was an attempt by the British Government to improve relations with the Irish Government and give them an advisory role in creating a form of governance for Northern Ireland that would be acceptable to all communities. Unionist/loyalist opposition was immediate and with a shocking level of violence. The Anglo-Irish Agreement guaranteed the principle of consent.

Conflict resolution is a natural progression from conflict settlement because it starts to address the root causes of the conflict. Resolution comes from building trust and new relationships between political opponents and creating forms of governance that help political adversaries to work together.

The Downing Street Declaration in 1993 built created a closer relationship between the British and Irish Governments. Talks were inclusive of all political parties, including those with paramilitary connections. Both the IRA and the Combined Loyalist Military Command called ceasefires and the journey towards the Belfast/Good Friday Agreement started. The Downing Street Declaration was co-signed by the British and Irish prime ministers who guaranteed the principle of consent. It was a good example of collaborative leadership.

Conflict transformation goes beyond identifying root causes and addresses the wider social, economic and political context in which the conflict started. A transformation can be observed through new thinking, new social and political systems, and new power dynamics and relationships. The Sunningdale Agreement in 1973 held great promise as a first stage in resolving the causes of the conflict and bringing republicans into negotiations. The British Government did not follow through on the Sunningdale Agreement and destroyed a fragile trust with republican leaders. Unionist leaders, shocked by the duplicity of British politicians, stayed on their guard and resisted further attempts to initiate power sharing in the Stormont Government. It took until 1993 and the Downing Street Declaration to persuade unionists that power sharing was key to bringing peace to Northern Ireland.

Lessons learned and the way forward

The common denominator in all four agreements was the principle of consent and with it came a commitment to protect the sovereignty of Northern Ireland. It is now clear that the ferocity of unionist resistance to power sharing with republicans, together with a lack of trust in the motives of the Irish Government, were major stumbling blocks to conflict resolution. Transformational and collaborative leaders were behind all four attempts at peacebuilding in 1975, 1985, 1993 and 1998 and their combined effects were cumulative and courageous.

When Sinn Féin won a general election in 2022, and local elections in 2023, the principle of consent brought the possibility of a united Ireland closer. The election results created an interesting political crossroad. From a republican perspective, there is an opportunity to lead the Executive, strengthen cross-party collaboration and restore the focus on peace. For unionists and loyalists, the consent principle is no longer the safety net it was. A recent comment by a leading unionist and co-founder of the DUP sums up the challenge:

> Unionism as a philosophy was always in many ways doomed because of Ireland's nature, the fact the North was carved off from the South. I do wonder at the future of the Union and I think we need to waken up [sic] and recognise that. We are in denial, constant denial.[10]

The British and Irish prime ministers were signatories to the Belfast/Good Friday Agreement and styled themselves as "third parties" to the peace process. Their leadership support of the negotiations helped to keep the process moving but the message was clear that the "heavy lifting" of peacebuilding now rested with the politicians in Northern Ireland. In 1998, US Senator George Mitchell's words spoke volumes:

> The organized [sic] violence of the past thirty years, which killed and maimed thousands, is over for now. Whether it is over for good depends on the people of Northern Ireland and their political leaders. I am hopeful that despite the inevitable human errors, they will conduct the affairs of Northern Ireland in a way that will build trust and confidence in the people.[11]

On reflection, the lack of precision in the final agreement complicated the early years of the peace process. Negotiations were focused on stopping violence and the political interests of the two major stakeholders: republican and unionist politicians. The outcome was a binding treaty but with no mechanism to resolve internal disputes between the dominant political parties.

The contribution of civil society

A clear sign of transformational change is when people feel safe to challenge the status quo. Conflict transformation is about creating a new future that supports peace rather than the reworking of the old fault lines and historical grievances. In Northern Ireland, the work of conflict transformation is not simply about addressing injustice through legislation, incentives or controls. It requires leaders who recognise that the emotional impact of long-term violent conflict may have a lasting effect on health and wellbeing and may endure over several generations. People stay connected to the past for a variety of reasons and none can be solved through legislation alone.

A crucial aspect of sustainable peace is the power of civil society. Community peace groups, development programmes and restorative justice initiatives create a reliable foundation for conflict transformation. These enterprises have been created and developed by transformational leaders who work through strong visions and values. They face a range of challenges from funding to staff burnout and even physical violence but they share a common purpose, and a deep concern for the future and a desire for sustainable peace. Leaders of grassroots organisations tend to be more authentic, informal and closer to both practical issues and how people feel.

Language and sustainable peace

In Northern Ireland, warrior discourse has traditionally been a recurring feature in both republican and unionist political speeches. The effect can be catastrophic: consider the behaviour of loyalist groups who listened to Ian Paisley (DUP) in November 1985 and who took his mantra "Never! Never! Never!" seriously and turned it into a rationale for political violence against Catholics.

Republican leaders frequently speak of their "patriot dead" and their "freedom fighters" at commemorations and funerals. This includes Sinn Féin leaders who grew to realise that peace in Northern Ireland was becoming a prerequisite for a united Ireland. Their peace discourses over the past 25 years have presented clear evidence of an internal political transformation, but their warrior language acted as a reminder of darker days. Sustainable peace is possible but it needs new peaceful discourses that reflect a shared vision of the future. Both unionist and republican forms of warrior discourses are linguistic and symbolic straitjackets which constrain the quality of dialogue needed by politicians and community leaders to build a society that is and feels safe.

The language of peace supports conflict transformation. The possibility of peace has both logical and emotional appeal. Warrior language impacts our fight/flight physiology which keeps us safe by preparing for threat. These are ancient responses from our highly efficient nervous system, and they help us to sense short-term excitement or danger depending on external circumstances. The language of peace connects with our human need to be social and safe. This is also a deeply embodied sense that tells us if we can trust someone and if we are in a safe environment. Conflict transformation and sustainable peace are possible when there are radical changes to the way leaders communicate and a greater appreciation of the damage caused by their warrior discourse. The Belfast/ Good Friday Agreement created a blueprint for peace in Northern Ireland, but it did not provide a leadership manual on how to do it, the language to use or the behaviours to display.

Leadership and sustainable peace

Political stakeholders and their leadership contributions

The collaborative leadership of two prime ministers, Bertie Ahern (Irish) and Tony Blair (British) was overall a positive contribution to the dynamics. Both individuals brought energy and the political will to end the violence. Bill Clinton provided consistency as a supporter of peace and a powerful voice as the US president. US Senator George Mitchell chaired the talks using structure and protocols to hold a diverse group of protagonists to account during months of difficult conversations. His leadership contribution was grounded in a belief that negotiations should not be destabilised by threats or acts of violence. Jonathan Powell, as chief British negotiator, brought practical experience of conflicts across the world and commanded respect from all participants. An experienced negotiator, his leadership style was both strategic and collaborative with a determination to keep people talking.

John Hume (SDLP) and David Trimble (UUP) both shared a strong desire for peace and influenced the negotiations with a more strategic approach. Sinn Féin leaders Martin McGuinness and Gerry Adams joined peace talks in September 1997 and quickly demonstrated their political skills. They were able to persuade the IRA to call a cessation to violence and were granted entry in accordance with the Mitchell Principles. While reports of the 1997–1998 talks reveal long, factious sections, there was movement in terms of conflict resolution.

The negotiations revealed layers of complexity as the deep-rooted distrust between unionist and republican leaders entangled other stakeholders, including the British and Irish Governments, in circular debates and broken promises. All parties to the conflict had their own political interests and supporters, which meant communications were frequently "playing to the crowd" tactics. In theory, the priority for peace building was the creation of a stable Northern Ireland Government with a democratic mandate and consensus on power sharing. While the Mitchell principles provided a sound basis for negotiations, the mission of securing peace for Northern Ireland was frequently overlooked in favour of tactical game-playing.

Backchannels and talking

An interesting development was the scale of informal communications between various parties to the peace process. A subtle form of peace building took place in secret talks, meetings and backchannels over several years before the Good Friday Agreement. Republican leaders had become experienced in this form of discreet contact and it is now public knowledge that a backchannel with the British Government had existed since the early 1970s.

In 1990, this backchannel was activated and operated as a "pipeline for messages" regarding a political and peaceful resolution of the conflict in Northern Ireland. Documentation from both republicans and the British Government indicated a genuine desire for peace from both sides. With the intervention of third parties, it is clear that in the early stages significant time and effort were placed on building relationships, establishing trust and ensuring tight safety and confidentiality. All parties faced physical danger and significant reputational risk from their constituents.

There are lessons to be learned about the role of backchannels in a peace process. When formal negotiations stall, they offer an opportunity to move a peace negotiation forward by building relationships and acts of trustworthiness, which may not otherwise be possible. Informal methods of communication, especially face to face, can create a different dynamic to the mechanics of formal negotiations. However, there are challenges that inevitably arise when there is a breach of trust or leak of confidential information and the "sounding board" advantage of the backchannel is lost through clumsy communication.

Relational leadership and bicycles

Jonathan Powell, as Chief Negotiator used his "bicycle theory" when negotiations became tense or participants threatened to walk out of sessions. He believed that it was vital to keep everyone talking and keep the wheels turning, however slowly.[12]

"Constructive ambiguity" was a negotiating approach that helped to create common ground prior to agreement but it did not create the relationships or longer-term conditions needed for sustainable peace. In the various accounts of the events, there is a level of vagueness about the quality of trust and confidence building between participants prior to settling down to negotiations. It is interesting to study George Mitchell's views on the importance of trust between chair and group members but we know less about how the level of trust between group members was managed. We know from his reflections that different factions spent a lot of time talking to him, complaining and not talking to each other.

It is also unclear whether participants shared a common purpose in negotiating peace for the whole of Northern Ireland or perceived themselves as representatives of different political factions. Unionists dominated the protocols agreed in the first six months of talks. Republicans were not present to contribute and this meant the Mitchell preconditions for peace talks reflected the political status quo of unionist domination. This brings us to another important aspect of sustainable peace. How were the people who disagreed with the terms of the final peace agreement managed and what happened next?

Spoilers and sustainable peace

The term "spoiler" is a term used to describe the resistance from individuals or groups opposed to a negotiated peace settlement.[13] Spoilers may disagree with political compromise especially if political elites and third parties have agreed to it. The Belfast/Good Friday Agreement is a good example of a negotiated settlement which promised to address the root causes but only partially resolved the issues. Spoilers have an important part to play because their responses are signalling a gap between the rhetoric of the peace settlement and the reality on the ground. From a transformational perspective, they are signalling where the barriers to sustainable peace exist. Historically, spoilers have been demonised, cast out or subjected to heavy state control. In Northern Ireland, opponents to the Belfast/Good Friday Agreement were labelled collectively as peace wreckers and dissidents.

Unfinished political business

Republican Sinn Féin (RSF) established in 1986 were horrified at the terms of the Belfast/Good Friday Agreement. The prospect of republican politicians sitting in a Northern Ireland Government was deeply offensive to them. Today, RSF continues to work politically for a united Ireland and to remove the influence of the British state from Northern Ireland:

> We condemn the political reformists who have turned their backs on the struggle for Irish freedom. The "peace process" has become more important than their stated long-term objective, a united Ireland.[14]

Saoradh, another republican organisation, was formed in 2016. They regard themselves as left-wing activists working for one Irish republic. Members do not contest elections because they view the Stormont Government as illegal. Ideologically, this group believes an Irish republic can be created through political activism. Their activity is under close scrutiny from the British security services:

> We extend fraternal best wishes to all those engaged in anti-imperialist, anti- colonial and revolutionary socialist struggles across the globe.[15]

Both republican groups argue that the Provisional Sinn Féin leadership accepted a political solution in 1998 that was well short of traditional republican ideology. Other examples of groups include the 32 County Sovereignty Movement established in 1997 and *Éirígí* in 2006. They all share traditional Irish republican principles.

The unionist mantra "It's right to say no" sums up the initial political reaction of the DUP and its leadership to the conditions of the Belfast/Good Friday Agreement. Twenty-five years later, some unionists believe that too many concessions were made to republicans. For them power sharing was seen as a flawed model; for republicans, it presented an opportunity to secure political power.

Going out of business

The Belfast/Good Friday Agreement set up conditions for decommissioning, but it did not end violence. In 2007, the Ulster Defence Association (UDA), the Ulster Volunteer Force (UVF) and Red Hand Commando (RHC) agreed to put their weapons beyond use. Since that date they have remained linked to violence, sectarian attacks and murders. The activities of loyalist spoiler groups are complex because while they are politically supportive of unionism, they are also involved in sectarian violence and a "rough justice" form of policing within their own communities.

The Provisional IRA (PIRA) agreed to a final decommissioning in 2005, two years before loyalist paramilitaries. At the time, some republican volunteers and veterans regarded this as a major betrayal. They reasoned that the Sinn Féin leadership had disbanded republican military capacity and lost critical political leverage. The fact that both the British state and loyalist groups continued to have armies was a bitter pill for republicans:

> No informer throughout the course of the conflict has been able to deal such a blow to the military capacity of the IRA as its own leadership has.[16]

Overnight republican decommissioning criminalised republican volunteers and veterans. Their presence and voice were a political headache for Sinn Féin. In the decade following, the term "dissident" emerged to label republican individuals and groups critical of Sinn Féin's political strategies. Decommissioning is a complex psychological and practical process for all stakeholders that requires an act of faith by the leaders involved. This statement from the Independent Monitoring Commission illustrates fundamental differences between republican and loyalist paramilitary organisations:

> One striking feature of the changes we have described has been how PIRA, however slowly, transformed itself under firm leadership and has gone out of business as a paramilitary group while loyalist groups, lacking comparable direction, have struggled to adapt.[17]

Terrorists or patriots?

A critical issue for sustainable peace is what happens to the soldiers once the war is over. From a republican perspective, volunteers had fought for nearly three decades believing the goal was a united Irish Republic. The act of decommissioning was a shocking experience for some IRA volunteers. Their own leaders had betrayed them by agreeing to weapons disposal before a British withdrawal, and before a loyalist decommissioning. The statement below reflects an intelligent and tragic assessment of the republican "Long War":

> The IRA was a manifestation of insurrectional energy within a nationalist community at that time, a reaction to how the British Army behaved. The difference between what was on offer in 1974 and what was accepted in 1998 did not justify the loss of one single life.[18]

During the peace process, IRA volunteers and veterans were marginalised and demonised by the media and their old comrades. For some individuals, their discontent with Sinn Féin's handling of decommissioning was channeled into forming new groups, which in 2016 merged into the New IRA. The New IRA believes that they are the custodians of Irish republican ideology and accepted responsibility for Lyra McKee's death in 2019. The logic for their continued existence is laid out in political terms but their actions brought condemnation and damage to their cause:

> You think this is madness? There will be madness as long as there is an armed occupation in Ireland. Go back to what the IRA did in the 1970s. Condemning the IRA is nothing new.[19]

Both armed loyalists and republicans represent a considerable threat to sustainable peace in Northern Ireland. The ongoing activity of the New IRA brings reputational damage for Sinn Féin's ambitions in mainstream politics. Both loyalist and republican paramilitary organisations recruit their members from their own communities and their activity ensures that new generations become entangled in violence whether political, or criminal, including drug related activities.

Tyranny of loyalty

Membership of a group fulfils primal needs for safety and relationships. Recruitment into both republican and loyalist paramilitary organisations has been fostered through history, peer pressure and loyalty to a noble cause. New generations taking up the fight to either defend the union or unite Ireland are influenced by warrior language and historic sectarian hatred.

The Belfast/Good Friday Agreement brought political negotiations to a close but failed to plan effectively for the emotional work of bringing peace. Peace spoilers are a natural consequence of a peace treaty and a lasting reminder that the root causes of the conflict have not been resolved. Their resistance is expressed politically, as members of paramilitary groups and street violence. A command and control approach to legislation or policing is unlikely to create a culture that supports sustainable peace.

The development of forgiveness and reconciliation, restorative justice and non- violent communication are just a few examples of the collaborative work that is being done to soften old divisions and bring emotional healing. These themes will be explored in more detail in Chapter four

Chapter summary

The Belfast/Good Friday Agreement was an important first step in securing a lasting peace but it is clear that the sovereignty of Northern Ireland was not the only issue. The polarisation between the notion of united Ireland and a United Kingdom dominated the peace negotiations and set the tone for the political reality of power sharing. Since 1998, there have been glimpses of collaborative leadership and its impact on the effectiveness of power sharing. The influence of British and Irish Governments in bringing a diverse group of political stakeholders to the negotiating table did help to produce a workable peace treaty. The brief collaborative work of the "Chuckle Brothers" is another example of what is possible if political leaders in Northern Ireland are willing to take a risk.

A source of hope for sustainable peace is the political work of middle ground political parties and particularly the Alliance Party which champions collaboration across traditional political and religious divisions. Power sharing in practice may be in a critical state but the middle ground of politics is having an impact on integrated education, marriages and collaborative activity across communities.

The work of community organisations represents a beacon of hope in the power of collaborative leadership. Individuals and groups have come together to break down barriers and respond to the needs of their communities. Many of these groups have collaborative leaders who share a clear vision and strong values with their supporters and volunteers. Many of these groups are working to soften the traditional divide of unionism and republicanism.

However, the continued presence of sectarian violence fueled by groups such as the New IRA and Real UFF is a strong indicator that communities in Northern Ireland remain divided along sectarian lines. The erection of "peace walls"[20] may help people to feel safer but they represent partition by another means. The legacy of the partition of Ireland in 1921 lives on.

One of the issues is that the root causes of conflict are communicated through stories, metaphors and symbolic language. The peace treaty may provide legislation for change but a lack of progress on implementation of terms of the agreement traps people and politicians into past grievances. A peace process represents an imagined future and is therefore unknown whereas the past is well known, albeit often contested.

In Northern Ireland the language of war has been instrumental in obstructing the peace process, but the language of peace has been equally problematic because it brings with it a perception that stakeholder needs and interests will be compromised. Collaboration does not mean compromise or surrender. Collaborative leaders acknowledge diverse views as sources of knowledge, skills and resources to be used to build common ground and generate solutions.

Notes

1. Cochrane, F. (2003) *The Reluctant Peace,* New Haven and London, Yale University Press, p. 241.
2. Mitchell, G. (1999) *Making Peace: The inside story of the making of the Good Friday Agreement,* London, William Heinemann, p. 187.
3. Mitchell, G. (1999) *Making Peace: The inside story of the making of the Good Friday Agreement,* London, William Heinemann, p. 57.
4. Ward, C. (2001) *Irish People,* 15 February.
5. Paisley,I.(2007)<http://cain.ulst.ac.uk/issues/politics/docs/dup/ip080507.htm>, 8 May.
6. McGuinness, M. (2007) <http://news.bbc.co.uk/1/hi/northern_Ireland/6636227.stm>,
7. McGuinness, M. (2014) *Belfast Telegraph*,15 September, p. 1.
8. McGuinness, M. (2016) *Belfast Telegraph,* 9 February.
9. O'Doherty, M. (2023) *How to fix Northern Ireland*, London, Atlantic Books, p. 131.
10. Wallace Thompson reported in the *Belfast Telegraph*, 7 September 2023.
11. Mitchell, G. (1999) *Making Peace: The inside story of the making of the Good Friday Agreement,* London, William Heinemann, p. 187.
12. Powell, J. (2008) *Great Hatred, Little Room: Making Peace in Northern Ireland*, London, Vintage, p. 322.

13. Stedman, S.J. (1997) Spoiler problems in Peace Processes, *International Security*, 22 (2).
14. Republican Sinn Fein (2023) Easter message, Republican *SINN FEIN Phoblacht*, 6 April, p. 1.
15. Saoradh New Year Statement reported in *Irish Republican News*, 1 January 2023.
16. McIntyre, A. (*2008*) *Good Friday: The Death of Irish Republicanism*, New York: Ausubo Press, p. 75.
17. Nolan, P. (2012) *Northern Ireland Peace Monitoring Report Number One*, Community Relations Council, Belfast, p. 46.
18. McIntyre, A. (2019) Shadow of a gunman featured in *Belfast Telegraph*, 29 April.
19. Mooney, J. (2019) Interview with New IRA, *Sunday Times*, 28 April.
20. This topic will be expanded upon in Chapter 4. This article is a good read.
    Alcaraz, T.G. (2023) Belfast has more peace walls now than 25 years ago, *theconversation.com*, 10 May.

CHAPTER 3

Transformational leadership

Reflections and insights

In Chapter 2, collaborative leadership was explored using the Belfast/Good Friday Agreement as a case study. The "constructive ambiguity" of peace talks brought political changes which included power sharing and a binding principle of consent. With international support and the signatures of two Prime Ministers, British and Irish, the Northern Ireland peace process appeared to be off to a positive start.

However, it was "constructive ambiguity" which has largely contributed to the unfinished political business between the two major traditions of unionism and republicanism. 25 years later, the ongoing divisions between political leaders continue to threaten the development of the new devolved government established in 2024.

In 2022 Sinn Féin won a general election that was followed in 2023 with a significant victory in local elections. The "safety net" role of the consent principle changed overnight and now represents a threat to unionists and loyalists. For republicans, there is a political opportunity to press on with Irish unity, and now with greater leadership power. From a whole system perspective there is an opportunity for Sinn Féin to lead Northern Ireland closer to sustainable peace but there are risks to be managed, internally from republicans and externally from politicians opposed to a united Ireland. Success in elections is no guarantee of political success in government but the political development of Sinn Féin is an interesting story of transformation within republicanism.

In this chapter, the political rise of Sinn Féin will be examined to understand how their leaders transformed the party and the republican movement. This will provide a context to evaluate the capability and resilience of current republican leaders to unite politicians and take Northern Ireland into an era of sustainable peace.

Transformational change and leadership

In terms of political development and radical internal change, Sinn Féin have travelled much further in the past 50 years than any of the other political parties in Northern Ireland. Since the 1970s there have been significant moments of transformational change in republicanism, which are documented but not necessarily fully understood.

Sinn Féin's transformational and peace discourses were well established by 2000. In the extract below from 1998, Gerry Adams was addressing his republican critics, but his language indicated a clear strategic perspective on the peace process:

> Republicans have to be long-headed and strategic in our approach. We are the ones who want maximum change. Sinn Féin is the one party who wants to see a total transformation of the situation, so we have to be patient, resolute and magnanimous.[1]

In 2023, for the first time in the history of Northern Ireland, republicans gained a majority in the Stormont Government. Past and present Sinn Féin leaders have consistently demonstrated a "long-headed" approach and recognise that their polling successes will continue to draw strong reactions from the DUP. An interesting question remains. How committed is the current Sinn Féin leadership to reach out to unionists, create a shared vision of sustainable peace and resist the temptation to push ahead, too soon with Irish unity?

Previous Sinn Féin leaders, Gerry Adams and Martin McGuinness, developed a track record of a collaborative approach in their backchannel activities and discrete peace talks. The history of their involvement in the political development of Sinn Féin also provides a practical case study of transformational leadership.

An early sign of a strategic approach from the Sinn Féin leadership goes back to the 1970s when the republican movement in the North was engaged in their "Long War". The extract below reveals a subtle reference to backchannel peace talks with the British Government, and the inevitable unionist resistance to the terms of the Sunningdale Agreement in 1973:

> Any call for peace, regardless of the sincerity of those involved which singles our republican violence and which ignores the nature of the society in which we live, is doomed to failure.[2]

At the time, the Army Council and senior IRA leaders were the dominant republican players and decision makers. Sinn Féin was regarded as a junior political wing and this meant a political route to Irish unity was largely a theoretical exercise. The position of PIRA's Chief of Staff was unequivocal:

> The Irish republic was proclaimed by the only way possible, by force of arms and only by force of arms can the Republic we seek be established.[3]

Throughout the 1970s, and behind the scenes, Gerry Adams was developing political strategies to bring social, economic and political equality to nationalist communities in Northern Ireland. He was convinced that empowering communities could change the inequality embedded in the social system. Two of the biggest hurdles to his political visions were the republican principles of abstention and physical force.

Sacred flame of abstention and mantle of physical force[4]

To understand the two major republican principles of abstention and physical force we need to go back to 1916 and the Easter Rising against British rule in Ireland. There were several immediate repercussions immediately after the Easter Rising which continue to impact Northern Ireland politics today. In 1918, Sinn Féin won a decisive victory in a general election in Dublin and established the first Irish Parliament (Dáil Éirean) in 1919. This parliament was outlawed but continued to meet in secret and did not recognise the legitimacy of the British Government to rule Ireland. The principle of abstention remains a republican principle and reflects an Irish republican perception that the partition of Ireland was an illegal act of a rogue state. To this day, elected Sinn Féin politicians do not take up their seats in the Westminster Parliament.

The British Government was under international pressure to grant home rule to Ireland but faced fierce opposition from a Protestant majority in the North. The result was the partition of Ireland in 1920 into 26 counties in the south and 6 counties in the north. In republican eyes partition legitimised the use of physical force against the British "occupation" of a part of Ireland. The principles of abstention and physical force are an important backcloth to this exploration of the political development of Sinn Féin and the scale of change facilitated by its leaders.

On 28 July 2005 Gerry Adams announced that "The war is over" and that the Provisional IRA (PIRA) was in the final phase of decommissioning. His statement represented a seismic change for the republican movement because the partition of Ireland had not ended and physical force had been abandoned. It became a political imperative for Sinn Féin to ensure that the physical force tradition was acknowledged and respected. Sinn Féin leaders realised that a narrative that PIRA volunteers had fought a noble war and the Army Council had chosen to decommission was more likely to keep republicans united.

Today, Sinn Féin politicians continue to honour the sacrifices made by PIRA veterans, their families and communities through commemorative ceremonies and rituals. The media have consistently reported this as a sign that republicans have not abandoned physical violence.

It was critical for the political ambitions of Gerry Adams and Martin McGuinness that they avoided damaging splits within the republican movement. Both were aware that decommissioning was seen internally as an ultimate betrayal of Irish republicanism. The republican transformation from armed to unarmed struggle was largely due to the "long-headedness" of Sinn Féin leaders and their influence with PIRA. It was a long and tortuous political journey.

The collapse of the Sunningdale Agreement in 1973 had been a pivotal moment for both Sinn Féin and PIRA. Republican leaders had agreed a ceasefire in return for improved conditions for their "prisoners of war". The ceasefire proved to be a catastrophic strategy for republicans because the British Government failed to deliver the promises made in the Sunningdale Agreement. Republicans were catapulted into a damaging split and the Provisional republican movement broke away. Previously the republican power base had operated from Dublin in the Irish Republic. Gerry Adams and Martin McGuinness took control of republican activities in North Ireland and made the removal of the British presence from Northern Ireland the focus of both military and political activities. The aftermath of the Sunningdale Agreement undoubtedly impacted republican attitudes to ceasefires and left PIRA highly suspicious of the trustworthiness of British politicians.

Gerry Adams and Martin McGuinness remained in power until 2017 and led several important transformations within the republican movement. They challenged the principle of abstention in the aftermath of republican hunger strikes in 1981. Their proposal to permit Sinn Féin to contest elections in Northern Ireland was communicated as another "battle front" in the war with the British. It was a skilful leadership move which laid the ground for later transformations in republican strategy. To the outside world, their ongoing use of warrior discourse trapped them in the one-dimensional label of "terrorists".

Sinn Féin and backchannels

From the early 1970s, Gerry Adams and Martin McGuinness, despite their proximity to the republican armed struggle, were actually getting a master class in how the British Government viewed "The Troubles" and specifically how to negotiate with British officials. Both Gerry Adams and Martin McGuinness were privy to secret peace talks between senior republicans and the British Government. The inner workings of the backchannel gave Gerry Adams and Martin McGuinness first-hand experience of the public face of the British Government and how its representatives operated in private. The talks were conducted discreetly in both Northern Ireland and London.

This early attempt at peace highlights a fundamental difference between republicans and the British Government. For republicans, an offer to ceasefire was a negotiating tactic to push an opponent into peace talks. The British Government viewed a ceasefire as a prerequisite to engaging in talks or negotiations especially on the issue of power sharing. In the years following the Belfast/Good Friday Agreement the precise timing of PIRA decommissioning brought several crisis points largely initiated by both unionist politicians and internal republican critics of Sinn Féin's strategy. The ability of Martin McGuinness to command respect with senior republicans on the Army Council and broker critical decisions on decommissioning undoubtedly prevented a major return to violence between 1998 and 2005.

Back in the 1970s and 1980s, Gerry Adams and Martin McGuinness walked a political tightrope as they developed Sinn Féin into a credible political entity. Their political discourses from 1976 reflect the complexity of the relationship between Sinn Féin and PIRA, and confirm that Sinn Féin saw a bigger political picture. Gerry Adams writing from his prison cell in Long Kesh:

> Revolutionary violence, and this includes sectarian violence, must be controlled and disciplined – symbol of our people's resistance and the spearhead for a peaceful and just society.[5]

The British backchannel with republicans continued to exist throughout the 1970s and 1980s and generally through the efforts of third parties dedicated to bringing peace to Northern Ireland. Despite the reputational damage of republican violence, third parties stayed focused on keeping a line of communication open. For example, the "channel" became active in December 1980 during the first republican hunger strike and was used to transmit messages between Martin McGuinness, PIRA and the British Government. During the period of two hunger strikes in 1980 and 1981 secret negotiations took place which signalled the republican leadership were ready to compromise and end the hunger strike if the British Government moved on prisoners' demands. Margaret Thatcher, the British Prime Minister, was aware of the channel but chose to take a hard line and refused to negotiate with "terrorists".

Through the 1980s Gerry Adams and Martin McGuinness gradually transformed the political direction of northern Irish republicans from armed to unarmed strategies. It was a careful and subtle exercise to persuade the majority of republicans to accept that a united Ireland could be achieved by political means. In transformational terms it was a series of slow steps, building support and a lot of talking.

For a backchannel to exist for two decades is evidence that all stakeholders privately shared a commitment to exploring a route to peace. In "Setting the record straight" published on 5 January 1994, Gerry Adams and Martin McGuinness published a comprehensive rebuttal of media reports that the British Government was not in peace talks with Sinn Féin. It all stemmed from the 1 November 1993 when the British Prime Minister, John Major, declared in parliament that the prospects of talks with Gerry Adams would "turn my stomach". This level of duplicity was a step too far for Sinn Féin leaders and they chose to break their silence on the existence of the backchannel:

> Over the past weeks many of you have asked Sinn Féin to provide proof of contact between us and representatives of the British Government. Up to now we have declined to do so in an attempt to protect the line of communication which has always been dependent on confidentiality and which we had hoped could assist in the search for a stable peace process.[6]

The content and quality of the republican rebuttal was testimony to detailed notes and minutes taken on all secret contacts with British officials and third parties. A weakened British Prime Minister working with a slim majority needed the political support of unionist MPs. It proved to be another tipping point for Sinn Féin in the long road to peace and from 1994 onwards Martin McGuinness insisted on direct contact with the British Government.

Armalite and ballot box

A speech in 1981 by Danny Morrison, Sinn Féin publicity director, is credited with shifting the internal republican dynamic towards mainstream politics. His words resonated with a republican audience and created the possibility of a dual strand strategy going forward:

> Who here really believes we can win the war through the ballot box? But would anyone object if, with a ballot box in one hand and an Armalite in the other, we take power in Ireland?[7]

A small step in the transformation of republican culture towards a political solution to Irish unity had been taken but it paradoxically legitimised further violence and that is what the world witnessed. On 20 July 1982, IRA bombs killed 11 soldiers and maimed seven military horses in Hyde Park in London. While Gerry Adams was proving successful at the "ballot box" and gaining a seat in the British parliament, he was under pressure internally to demonstrate that he had not abandoned the physical force tradition. The traditional principles were constraining his efforts to persuade republicans that a peaceful political route was the only way forward. From a Sinn Féin perspective, the two republican principles of abstention and physical force were becoming a straitjacket that confined republicans to a political wilderness.

The outside world continued to view the relationship between Gerry Adams, Martin McGuinness and the IRA as a dangerous combination. Internally, the two leaders were engaged in a risky political juggling act of leading Sinn Féin towards mainstream politics without triggering internal splits in the republican movement:

> We have created a dynamic for change. We go into the next phase of struggle armed only with our political ideas.[8]

This statement is an interesting combination of transformational discourse and warrior language. In the one short statement above, we are shown how much internal political juggling Sinn Féin leaders were engaged in.

We now know that Gerry Adams was engaged in discreet talks with John Hume, the SDLP leader in the 1980s. This relationship represented the start of a nationalist coalition, which consisted of SDLP, Sinn Féin, the Irish Government and supporters in the USA. This collaboration acted as a foundation for the Downing Street Declaration in 1993 and joint statements indicated that both John Hume and Gerry Adams wanted to secure justice and equality for nationalist communities and bring peace to Northern Ireland. Both men recognised the need to reassure unionists that peace could be brought about by a shared political will. Around this time Sinn Féin leaders started to sow the seeds for another republican transformation and one that would require a collaborative approach with Protestants and unionists:

> Since our last Ard Fheis, I have had a series of discussions with Northern Ireland Protestants. These discussions crystallised for me the need for republicanism to understand the perceptions and fears of this section of our citizens.[9]

Within days of this speech PIRA bombed a Remembrance Day parade at Enniskillen. The intention was to target British soldiers and security personnel but the positioning of the bomb caused a gable end wall to collapse and 10 civilians were killed and 63 people injured. It was not an internal response to the political direction that Sinn Féin leaders were taking but a mistake on the ground that brought international outrage.

The experience of the Hume-Adams talks confirmed to Gerry Adams what he already knew: a military solution would not bring Irish unity. The Enniskillen bomb brought serious reputational damage to the republican cause but that did not stop IRA operations. The next big challenge for Sinn Féin was to find a way to close down the "armalite" strategy and push on with winning at the ballot box.

Republicans and constitutional politics

By the early 1990s a major transformation of republican ideology was underway and it would legitimise Sinn Féin's role in constitutional politics in Northern Ireland. This was a very challenging time for republicans because they were being asked to accept that partition would not be immediately reversed, and the British influence in Northern Ireland would remain. The military campaign conducted by PIRA had not driven the British state out of Ireland which meant Sinn Féin leaders needed to work quickly to protect republican interests and keep the IRA engaged with a peace strategy.

Gerry Adams adopted transitional discourses that were a more sophisticated version of the "armalite and ballot" mantra but they served an important purpose, to prepare the republican movement for existential change:

> We are often more successful when we have a flexible approach. We are at our weakest when we are forced into a static political position where the more powerful forces of imperialism can be employed to isolate us.[10]

In 1993 the British side of the backchannel was adamant that face to face peace talks with Sinn Féin could only take place if the IRA called a permanent ceasefire. Martin McGuinness managed to persuade the IRA to hold a two-week ceasefire from the 10 May 1993. This was a remarkable example of transformational leadership in the context of previous unproductive ceasefires in 1972, 1975 and 1980–81.

Martin McGuinness, as senior republican leader, was obliged to follow PIRA protocols and seek permission for ceasefires from the republican leadership, the Army Council. Sinn Féin leaders remained loyal to the republican cause but learned to adapt quickly to changing external circumstances, win elections and become sharp negotiators. In the years the backchannel existed they warned successive British Governments of the long-term damage of republican splits and the state of readiness of PIRA for change.

Sinn Féin become peace builders

In public John Major, the British Prime Minister, continued to press Sinn Féin for the surrender of PIRA weapons in return for a place at peace talks. There is an inevitability in the response from Gerry Adams to republicans in 1994:

> One has to ask does anyone really expect the IRA to cease its activities so that British civil servants can discuss with Sinn Féin the surrender of IRA weapons after we have been decontaminated? [sic][11]

The Sinn Féin leadership knew that republicans resented being demonised and backed into a corner especially in a conflict scenario where armed loyalists and British soldiers continued to operate on the streets of Northern Ireland. Gerry Adams countered arguments over decommissioning by focusing on the political issue of consent. He reiterated his support for the principle of consent and reasoned that unionists could not and should not be coerced into a united Ireland. A split in PIRA in 1993 would have been a disaster and destroyed the careful backstage sequencing of dialogue between Sinn Féin leaders and the Army Council. In 2023 newly released State papers prove how much both British and Irish Governments relied on the Sinn Féin leadership, at the time describing them as "the last hope for progress" and "irreplaceable".[12]

Between 1994 and 1995 Sinn Féin started to publish records of discussions with the British Government. "Towards a negotiated settlement" were three separate documents which clearly reveal that Sinn Féin leaders were committed to the peace process and a permanent removal of guns in Irish politics. In return, republicans wanted a political settlement that was inclusive, equitable and sustainable:

> What is required is an approach that creates political conditions in which for the first time, the Irish people can reach a democratic accommodation, in which the consent of nationalists and unionists can be achieved, in which a process of national conciliation and healing can begin.[13]

Martin McGuinness navigated his own transformation to the ballot box to become a senior political leader in the Northern Ireland Executive. In 2007, he became deputy First Minister and was in a prime position to continue influencing the peace process. His determination to make the peace process work can be seen in the way he consistently reached out to unionists and showed respect for their Queen. A historic handshake in 2012 was followed by his attendance at a state banquet at Windsor Castle in 2014:

> He said the Queen understood the significance of the peace process and the symbolism of the two of them shaking hands.[14]

Gerry Adams and Martin McGuinness proved that they were committed to bringing peace to Northern Ireland and demonstrated remarkable courage in persuading PIRA into a peaceful settlement and political route to Irish unity. Both men travelled a long way to gain their credibility as politicians and peacebuilders. The historical republican mission of a united Ireland has not been abandoned but in 2023 Sinn Féin stated priorities for Northern Ireland were to address the social, economic and political issues for all communities and bring sustainable peace. This political rhetoric implied that the ending of partition and the creation of a united Ireland had become secondary priority. It is a rational transformative strategy that delivers a coherent political message but to traditional republican groups such as Republican Sinn Féin, this represents a "downgrading" of the historic dual goal of a united Ireland and the removal of British influence on the island.

The language of peace

Initially Gerry Adams and Martin McGuinness talked about peace discreetly within the republican movement but as their confidence grew their peace discourses entered the public domain. By 1987 Sinn Féin had published "Scenario for Peace" which proposed greater cooperation between nationalist and unionist politicians and demonstrated that republicans were willing to step outside their traditional agenda in the interests of peace. Later in 1992 "Towards Lasting Peace" revealed a shift in the traditional republican demand for British withdrawal and with it a subtle change in relationship with the British Government.

Throughout the 1990s Sinn Féin's communication with unionists became more inclusive with language drawn from the work of the Truth and Reconciliation Commission in South Africa, an organisation established in 1996 to promote restorative justice as part of the post-apartheid peace building.

Republicans retained close links with parties involved in a number of international conflicts and used these relationships to strengthen their "moral high ground" discourse as a means to influence a range of stakeholders in the merit of the republican cause:

> The international experience of conflict resolution teaches us the way forward is through equality of treatment and inclusive negotiations without preconditions. The British Government and the leaders of unionism know this also.[15]

Further development of Sinn Féin peace discourses can be tracked through an increasing use of the word "we" and symbolic acts of respect. New language appeared in speeches e.g. "Language of Invitation", a term used by Tom Hartley, a Sinn Féin politician. Throughout the 1990s he engaged with and promoted cross-community peace initiatives and advocated the power of forgiveness and reconciliation:

> Republicans want not more suffering, no more victims. That is why we are irrevocably committed to the peace process.[16]

A transformational act of leadership can be observed when Mayor Alex Maskey, a republican, laid a wreath at a British Legion remembrance event in 2002. It was described as a "remarkable and graceful act of individual reconciliation" and demonstrated that small acts and symbolic gestures have an important role to play in conflict transformation. The acts of leadership shown by Tom Hartley and Alex Maskey contributed to a powerful moral high ground for the Sinn Féin peace strategy because their actions matched their political rhetoric.

Martin McGuinness continued to prove himself a transformational leader during his time in office between 2007 and 2017. In 2007 Sinn Féin joined the Northern Ireland policing board and gained a voice in matters of law and order. The PSNI replaced the Royal Ulster Constabulary in

2001 as part of the reforms agreed in the Belfast/Good Friday Agreement in 1998. For some republicans the idea of Sinn Féin working with the PSNI to police Catholic communities was an unacceptable betrayal. From a traditional perspective republicans who had fought the British state were now policing their own communities on behalf of the British state. Those with long memories of police brutality towards Catholic communities found it difficult to reconcile with the direction Sinn Féin leaders were taking them. A decade later, some of the republican migrants from PIRA had regrouped and become a new paramilitary group that we now know as the New IRA. By 2016 Martin McGuinness was taking a hard line publicly towards armed republican groups aware of the reputational damage it brought to Sinn Féin politicians operating in the Stormont Government:

> The tiny number of people out there who are committed to violence, their strategy is really about trying to divide Sinn Féin from our unionist government.[17]

His reference above to "our unionist government" is an example of astute political courtesy that served to distance Sinn Féin politics from the violence of the New IRA and acknowledged that unionists held a majority in the Stormont Government. If we compare this to PIRA's Easter message ten years earlier it is clear that the Sinn Féin leadership had strong internal republican support for their political strategies and commitment to peace:

> The IRA has no responsibility for the tiny number of former republicans who have embraced criminal activity. The leadership of Óglaigh na hÉireann believes it is possible to achieve the republican goal of a united Ireland through the alternative route of purely peaceful and democratic means.[18]

Internal republican opposition to Gerry Adams and Martin McGuinness was not one homogenous group but coalitions of people who objected to the terms of the Belfast/Good Friday Agreement from a range of philosophical and political perspectives. For several decades the two men faced a mix of strong opposition, vitriolic criticism and demonisation from unionists, their loyalist supporters, British politicians and the media. The political trajectory of their leadership laid out in this chapter indicates they were visionary, quick learners and driven by the end goal of a united Ireland.

The Sinn Féin leadership and their legacy

The Sinn Féin peace strategy was based on a realisation that the republican "Long War" with the British state could not be won. A political turn towards peace would bring a moral high ground for republicans and be a perfect launch pad for a different form of interaction with unionists and the British Government. It also brought them international support from the Irish Diaspora in the USA.

The biggest challenge was not only to persuade PIRA to agree to a ceasefire but to persuade them to begin a ceasefire before peace talks commenced. Despite the historic legacy of republican physical force PIRA played their part in 2005 and decommissioned without a withdrawal of British troops and an agreed date for Irish unity. They made themselves redundant and gave Gerry Adams and Martin McGuinness the political advantage to complete the transformation of Sinn Féin into a democratically elected political force in Northern Ireland. The end date for a united Ireland remains as yet unknown.

In 2017, the two men passed their batons onto another generation of republicans with the realisation that their historical involvement with armed struggle could erode Sinn Féin's political aspirations in the future. At the time of writing Michelle O'Neill is First Minister of Northern Ireland and vice president of Sinn Féin. Mary Lou Macdonald is currently leader of the opposition in the Irish Dáil and President of Sinn Féin. Their relationship represents a powerful political coalition going forward. Two of the big leadership challenges for Michelle O'Neill are the opposition of the DUP and the response of minority republican groups, Her attendance as First Minister of Northern Ireland at the coronation of the British Monarch, King Charles III in 2023 proved highly controversial. The following quotes are drawn from the same publication:[19]

> Not only is this decision a complete abandonment of basic republican principles, it is a slap in the face of all who have suffered. (Irish Republican Socialist Party)
>
> The world knows the pain and suffering caused by the Crown Forces in Ireland. The new British King is responsible for the pain and suffering of so many people in the Six Counties. (Republican Sinn Féin)

These responses from rival republican political parties are less of a threat than DUP opposition but they illustrate the sheer scale of transformational change that Martin McGuinness and Gerry Adams achieved. In her rebuttal of critical remarks, Michelle O'Neill reasoned that she was representing the whole community of Northern Ireland It brought her positive feedback from unionist politicians who called her actions "a step in the right direction".

Northern Ireland and conflict transformation

In the previous chapter, conflict transformation was defined as an integrated approach which supports the structures, systems and relationships needed to bring about lasting societal change. Several key drivers impact conflict transformation and they include provision for immediate conflict prevention and the establishment of a self-sustaining political system. The Belfast/Good Friday Agreement addressed both these dimensions but without the full support and collaboration of political leaders on how to implement the terms of the agreement. Leadership behaviours and actions are the key to societal transformation and the creation of conditions for sustainable peace.

Whilst the "guns" are out of Northern Ireland politics some weapons remain in the hands of both loyalist and republican paramilitary groups. A major driver in conflict transformation is the capacity for reconciliation and healing within communities and this has proved to be a powerful role for grassroots and third sector organisations. The quality of leadership in these groups is a potential cornerstone for sustainable peace and will be explored in more detail in Chapter 5.

A major inhibitor for sustainable peace is the two competing traditions of unionism and republicanism which continue to dominate Northern Ireland politics. The power-sharing model agreed in 1998 makes it easy for one of the dominant parties to collapse the Executive. In the context of transformational leadership, this is a major challenge for the Northern Ireland Executive. It is clear that the current power-sharing model is a barrier to sustainable peace because it recreates old divisions and makes political work a continuous battle between traditions and identities. This issue is not the structure of power sharing and the solution is not a restructure. The solution lies in challenging the values, behaviours and language of the politicians engaged in power sharing. Another challenge is the continued presence of both republican and loyalist paramilitary groups which represent a clear signal that for some citizens the conflict in Northern Ireland is not over. The phenomenon of continued sectarian violence permeated by known armed groups and individuals both within and between communities will be explored in more detail in the next chapter.

A new generation of Sinn Féin leaders

Earlier in the chapter, a key question was posed on whether the current Sinn Féin leadership is capable of leading the devolved government and taking Northern Ireland into an era of sustainable peace. This is a good moment to draw together a number of themes on transformational leadership and evaluate how they apply to sustainable peace. From the case study of Sinn Féin political development, there was significant evidence of several major transformations in the republican movement and how the lessons learned by their leaders were applied to each new political opportunity. This legacy currently sits with Michelle O'Neill and her Sinn Féin colleagues who are now equipped with significant advantages and opportunities to influence a devolved government in Northern Ireland. They also face significant challenges.

Current advantages and strengths

- Sinn Féin have a track record of winning elections in both the Irish republic and Northern Ireland. Unlike unionists, the participation of northern republicans in elections and government is relatively new to them. Party activists in the 1980s and 1990s were on a rapid learning curve gaining practical experience of conflict resolution and constitutional politics.
- The cross-border bodies set up after the Belfast/Good Friday Agreement have laid a solid foundation for increasing cooperation between Northern Ireland and the Irish Republic.
- The case for a united Ireland is not simply a historical mission to end partition. There are sound economic, social and political reasons for Irish unity. Sinn Féin have consistently pointed out the inefficiencies of duplication with two governments, two police forces, two health services, two transport services etc.
- The moral high ground has proved a political advantage for republicans. Their political discourses have evolved over time from the language of freedom and injustice to the language of peace and forgiveness. Morally it is hard for their opponents to argue against human rights, democracy and respect.
- International interest has taught republicans the value of having support from outside Northern Ireland. In June 2023 Michelle O'Neill as First Minister designate visited the White House to draw attention to the US Government's commitment to the Belfast/Good Friday Agreement.

Current weak spots

- The Belfast/GoodFriday Agreement did not provide enough detail on how the political opponents would work together. There was no system of incentives to collaborate factored into the agreement and this has sustained a combative political dynamic that is damaging for good governance.

- A new generation of Sinn Féin politicians is only one generation away from violence. Michelle O'Neill has made it clear in public speeches that she is proud of her republican heritage, but it allows her detractors to link the activities of the New IRA to the work of Sinn Féin and this could bring reputational damage to her personally and to her role as First Minister.

Future opportunities

- The current republican electoral success represents historic change. In theory, the consent principle should facilitate a referendum and establish a "reality check" on the scale of support for ending partition.
- The Hume/Adams partnership taught Sinn Féin leaders that they could collaborate with other nationalists and achieve change without diminishing the republican legacy. There is an opportunity to reach out to the middle group parties and lead a more collaborative approach to political work.

Remaining challenges

- The legacy of republicanism remains a prominent feature of their Ard Fheis gatherings, Easter speeches and commemorations. The principles of abstention and physical force could impede future political development within Sinn Féin.
- Republican political parties faithful to the traditional principle of abstention remain an echo of the past but they still have a voice. The latest political group, Aontú, formed in 2019, present themselves as an all-Ireland party with a mission to "fix the political culture".
- New IRA members are now the self-styled custodians of republican principles. They act and behave as a paramilitary but are not averse to criminal activities to fund operations.
- An issue for the future is the continued abstention of elected republican politicians from the Westminster Parliament. This remains a

strong signal and a potential "Achilles' heel" for Sinn Féin political aspirations. DUP politicians vote in the Westminster Parliament.

Chapter summary: "Ourselves alone"[20]

It will be impossible to bring sustainable peace to Northern Ireland if the devolved government remains collapsed because it means the British Government takes control of the level of budget funding. This essentially disempowers the Executive to make spending decisions in the best interests of Northern Ireland citizens. All roads lead to effective power sharing and the development of new forms of leadership, which encourage collaboration and respect amongst political leaders in Northern Ireland. However, it will take a powerful and resourceful transformational leader to persuade the DUP to share power and collaborate in the best interests of all citizens in Northern Ireland.

Collaboration does not mean relinquishing power or being forced to like your political opponent or indeed someone who has been an enemy. In a collaborative relationship resources are shared, developed and grown. A good example can be seen in grassroots and third sector organisations who have traditionally competed for funding but increasingly they are learning to collaborate to deliver vital services.

In large organisational and social systems, senior leaders are discovering that traditional models of leadership are defunct in the face of the complex external challenges and cultural changes. Election successes have opened a door for republicans and the way they handle this power could now shape politics in Northern Ireland. Sinn Féin potentially faces another crucial transformation if they are to move from "ourselves alone" to collaborative cross-party politics. The current Sinn Féin leadership currently holds an important key to how the issue of Irish unity is managed and a new political culture created. It remains to be seen if Sinn Féin can step away from the past and lead the Executive into a new era of political collaboration and Northern Ireland closer to sustainable peace.

In the next chapter, trauma-informed leadership will be introduced as a contemporary form of leadership to address current social barriers to sustainable peace. The learning about leadership from the first three chapters will be applied to the current and future challenges facing political leaders in Northern Ireland.

Notes

1. Adams, G. (2000) Crossing the Rubicon, *Irish Republican News*, 18 May, p. 1.
2. Adams, G. (1976) The Long War, essay published by Republican Press Centre, p. 6.
3. MacStiofain, S. (1970) *An Phoblacht*, April, p. 1.
4. Adapted from O'Brien, B. (1995) *The Longest War: The IRA and Sinn Féin*, Dublin: O'Brien Press, p. 21.
5. Adams, G. (1976) The Long War, essay published by Republican Press Centre, p. 13.
6. Setting the record straight, 5 January 1994, published by *Sinn Féin*, 44 Parnell Square, Dublin.
7. Author notes from an interview with Danny Morrison, 2001.
8. Adams, G. (1986) Ard Fheis report, *An Phoblacht*, p. 1.
9. Adams, G. (1987) Ard Fheis report, An *Phoblacht*, 31 October, p. 1.
10. 82nd Ard Fheis report, *An Phoblacht*, 1986, p. 9.
11. Adams, G. (1994) Presidential Address, reported *An Phoblacht*, 26 February, p. 2.
12. McCullagh, D., McCarthy, J. & Ó Cionnaith, F. (2022) State paper: Threats to the embryonic Peace Process, RTÉ, 30 December, p. 1.
13. Adams, G. (1994) Presidential Address, *An Phoblacht*, 26 February, p. 1.
14. McDonald, H. (2014) Interview with Martin McGuinness "I like the Queen", *The Guardian,* 12 October, p. 1.
15. McGuinness, M. (1997) Wolfe Tone Commemoration, *An Phoblacht*, 22 June, p. 1.
16. Hartley, T. (1995) Ard Fheis speech, *An Phoblacht,* 25 February.
17. McGuinness, M. (2016) *Irish Republican News,* 26 March 2016.
18. Provisional IRA, Annual Easter Message, *Irish Republican News,* 13 April 2006.
19. O'Neill, M. (2023) Irish *Republican News*, 27 April, p. 2.
20. Sinn Féin means " We ourselves" but is frequently quoted as " Ourselves Alone".

CHAPTER 4

Trauma-informed leadership

Reflections and insights

Northern Ireland is engaged in a journey of conflict transformation. It started with the Belfast/Good Friday Agreement in 1998, and a partial resolution of the root causes of a civil conflict called "The Troubles". The agreement created the conditions for a power-sharing model of government with formal commitments to human rights, equality, economic and social justice, and wider community engagement. Conflict transformation is a process which is characterised by a focus on the future with new paradigms of thinking, systems and political dynamics.

Conflict transformation needs leaders with vision, long-term strategies and the ability to work for the "greater good" of the people they serve. In previous chapters, some of these leadership characteristics were discovered in community development organisations, projects and charities where the ability to collaborate with other stakeholders was essential. In the transformation of a society impacted by sectarian violence, small acts of collaborative leadership coupled with positive results can build confidence that sustainable peace is possible.

In May 2022 Sinn Féin gained a majority in the general election and the political dynamics of the Northern Ireland Government shifted as Michelle O'Neill, leader of Sinn Féin, became First Minister designate. This may have been a historic moment for republican politicians but it signified a clear threat for their unionist counterparts. There had been a unionist-led government in Northern Ireland since partition in 1921. The 2022 general election results brought the prospect of a united Ireland closer. Currently, Sinn Féin's political muscle in both Northern Ireland and the Irish Republic gives their politicians a significant opportunity to effect change in the way business is conducted in the power-sharing government. A major political challenge facing the Sinn Féin leadership will be to influence elected politicians to collaborate on urgent legislative and policy work. Michelle O'Neill is likely to face both internal republican expectations of a united Ireland and the predictable DUP opposition to any change to the sovereign status of Northern Ireland.

A major challenge facing all political leaders in Northern Ireland is that the credibility, authority and leadership capability of the Executive is weakened from repeating cycles of direct rule. An ancient political duality between allegiance to a "united Ireland" or a United Kingdom continues to dominate Northern Ireland's politics and impact the quality of cross-party dialogue and collaboration.

This chapter will continue to explore the role of transformational and collaborative leadership in the process of achieving sustainable peace. It will specifically examine the long-term effect violent conflict has on peace and use scientific evidence to develop a rationale for trauma-informed leadership. The impact of "The Troubles" on health and wellbeing will be explored and evidence presented on the link between transgenerational trauma and poor mental health. During "The Troubles" the word trauma was not a common term nor was it widely used to explain the long-term impact of violent conflict on individuals, families and communities. Although theory and practice in post-conflict trauma was an established field at the time of the Belfast/Good Friday Agreement, it was largely the domain of psychiatrists and psychologists.

Today, neuroscience is a well-established discipline which brings practical knowledge and tools to deepen an understanding of the physiological nature of trauma. This is a positive development because it opens up new approaches to healing and recovery that educate and empower people impacted by a variety of traumatic experiences.

Acts of leadership post-conflict

Trauma-informed acts of leadership can go a long way towards initiating post-conflict healing and they represent good practice in conflict resolution. In Northern Ireland there were acts of trauma-informed leadership before the term was common in mainstream health provision. Three recognisable forms are acts of apology, forgiveness and trust building. Below is an example of an act of apology from a Sinn Féin politician, Tom Hartley, in 1995:

> I have publicly acknowledged the hurt that republicans inflicted on others. I do so again today. For healing to work, everyone must do this. Republicans, unionists, loyalists and especially the British Government.[1]

An apology can de-escalate a conflict situation because it acknowledges that hurt was inflicted. Tom Hartley understood that his gesture might be misunderstood as empty words but he continued to work tirelessly for peace. He remained an advocate for forgiveness and reconciliation and became known for his "Language of Invitation" towards Protestant communities and political colleagues. Hartley served on Belfast City Council between 1993 and 2013, was Mayor of Belfast in 2008–9 and went on to gain respect across the political spectrum in Northern Ireland. An act of apology can be powerful if it is genuine because it speaks to our human need for dignity and safety, and helps to release both parties from a traumatising relationship or experience.

A powerful act of forgiveness was epitomised by Gordon Wilson's words "I bear no ill will, I bear no grudge". In 1987, he held his daughter's hand as she died under rubble resulting from a PIRA bomb during a Remembrance Day parade in Enniskillen. His calls for forgiveness and reconciliation led him to beg loyalist groups to desist from retaliatory violence. By 1989, Gordon Wilson had founded a charity called the "Spirit of Enniskillen" and developed an integrated education programme for young Catholics and Protestants to travel outside Northern Ireland and then return to use their experiences to enhance cross-community relationships.

The ability to develop and sustain trust is an important component of conflict resolution, transformation and trauma healing. It generally involves taking some risks but can be an opportunity to establish a working relationship between conflicting parties. Acts of trustworthiness help to build a safer environment for people to engage in conflict resolution. Following violent conflict the negotiation process can be stressful and potentially volatile with a myriad of emotional and psychological responses. By creating a less threatening environment through acts of trustworthiness, it is possible to rebuild sufficient trust to navigate the tensions that may emerge during negotiations.

In Northern Ireland a current example of an act of trustworthiness can be seen in the work of loyalist veterans with young people engaged in conflict transformation initiatives and restorative justice schemes. The veterans "lived experience" of paramilitary violence and their commitment to build non-violent capacity in a younger generation is a well-documented but challenging endeavour:

> To ignore such people, sneer at their efforts to build a sustainable and peaceful future, or attempt to remove them from society because of their past criminality, may be counterproductive.[2]

The development of a trusting relationship has two major phases. Firstly, trust building by developing rapport and demonstrating respect, and secondly by completing small acts of trustworthiness. Once built, trust needs to be sustained through quality relationships, social interaction and delivering promises. Trust can be destroyed quickly if the trustworthiness of others is called into question but it can be repaired by acts of apology and forgiveness.

Acts of apology, forgiveness and trust building all contribute to conflict resolution and transformation. They also have an important role in trauma healing because they nourish our human need for dignity and respect and acknowledge the long-term effects of violent conflict. Symbolic gestures and language can also be powerful forms of healing but only if consistent actions follow. From a neuroscience perspective empty political gestures and statements are a wasted effort. Human beings have brains that are neurologically hard-wired to spot insincerity and danger.

It is interesting that the route to sustainable peace follows a similar process with a combination of relationship building, social interaction and delivering promises. In any study of how the Belfast/Good Friday Agreement was negotiated it is clear that there was less attention paid to the relational aspects of peacebuilding. The final agreement in 1998 reflected structural and procedural aspects of initiating peace but an opportunity was lost to recognise the traumatic impact of extended violent conflict had on families and communities, and indeed on the negotiators themselves.

Neuroscience and trauma

Human beings have major survival needs that include safety and social interaction. As mammals we become aware of danger (real or perceived) through a rapid signalling system between our brain stem and a network of nerves serving every cell in the body. Social interaction gives us an additional advantage because it brings more information about our safety. We use our five senses to absorb social cues about our environment and other people. Through social interaction we check if it is safe to trust others and whether we might feel more secure by working with others. We have the ability to consciously put out a social cue as a test to check if the other party is friendly or threatening.

In war, conflict or any frightening situation, our basic need for safety is disrupted and our nervous system reacts automatically to protect us. A specific traumatic event is experienced physiologically first as shock, and later through observable emotional, psychological or social cues. This means any form of threat, whether real or perceived, is experienced in the body as an individual and unique survival response. Where there is a low-level threat encountered by a steady state nervous system, a short activation will be followed by a return to steady state and the individual goes about their day. This can be experienced in the rapid sensations that flood the nervous system when a car driver ahead suddenly brakes. Moments later and after an automatic rapid response we carry on driving and our nervous system starts to go back to its steady state. This natural ebb and flow of our nervous system is an evolutionary advantage and a perfectly normal healthy response.

High threat environmental conditions such as war, extended conflict direct or indirect violence bring a very high level of activation in the fight/flight responses as the body's biology moves to protect the individual from threat. If the nervous system perceives a threat to life it will shut down all but essential functions and the individual may freeze. An efficient human system to detect threats is now switched on and without self-regulation can affect an individual's healthy responses in the future.

A semi-permanent "switched on" system can impact physical and mental health many years after the original experience especially if environmental conditions remain threatening. An extended violent conflict can result in traumatic experiences for both adults and children. The difference is that children have less capacity to understand intellectually what is happening to them so the impact of trauma is more likely to be felt within their bodies:

> Infants and children are the most vulnerable as their brains and bodies are still developing. Witnessing an explosion or running to a shelter – in contrast to ongoing familial neglect or abuse – is primarily physiological rather than psychological.[3]

It is important to remember that our immediate response to a threat is automatic and we are not immediately able to detect whether the threat is real. With a calm physiological state we "feel" safe and this is reflected in our relationships with others. With an activated physiological state there are fewer cues of safety and in extreme circumstances such as war or violent conflict, an individual may remain in survival mode indefinitely. This can be complicated by the way traumatic experiences are communicated within families and communities. Responses can range from "silence" to repetitive "storytelling". Silence may be an individual's coping mechanism to manage painful memories but other family members, especially children, can sense it. Storytelling may bring short-term solace for an individual but there is a possibility of trauma transmission to family members.

Trauma is a human response, not an illness

Trauma is a natural human response to any unusual, unexpected or overwhelming event that leaves us feeling helpless. Our responses to traumatic experiences or environments are therefore a biological strength and not a mental weakness to be overcome. This is a fundamental consideration for the way mental health is perceived. Neuroscience has given us a biological understanding of how both our minds and bodies respond to a threat and retain a memory of the experience. It also explains why a traumatic memory can continue to manifest itself as images, physical senses and dark thoughts.

In an extended and/or violent conflict people are subjected to repeating patterns of shock and terror. The possibility of death, whether real or perceived, will automatically initiate a state of freeze or dissociation and important senses such as seeing, hearing, speech and memory may be temporarily impaired. This has important implications for both trauma healing and conflict transformation. A fragment of a traumatic memory may stay in the mind and body for several decades and be masked by a range of coping mechanisms including silence, alcohol and prescription or illicit drugs.

Trauma symptoms are not necessarily linked to a single event and the following criteria reflect the pervasive nature of trauma and why it can have an impact on mental health:[4]

- Exposure to actual or threatened death, serious injury or sexual violence. This includes a direct experience of threat or as a witness.
- Learning that a close friend or relative was exposed to a violent event or accident.
- Indirect exposure to the impact of trauma by professionals such as first responders.

These definitions help to explain the long-term, hidden impact of trauma on physical and mental health. We now know that conditions such as anxiety, depression and post-traumatic stress disorder (PTSD) can be the result of exposure to physical, psychological or emotional violence.

The unbearable heaviness of remembering

Between 1920 and 1921, the partition of Ireland, the creation of Northern Ireland and the subsequent creation of a republic of Ireland had a devastating effect on Catholic communities in the new northern province. Northern Ireland became part of the United Kingdom. A line drawn on a map split Catholic communities and added to the sectarian tension that already existed between Catholics and Protestants. This was a major collective traumatic experience and one which over time is likely to have contributed to the root causes of the "The Troubles". Irish republicans found themselves living in a society dominated by unionists and Protestants, and for their political activists and military volunteers, Irish freedom became a sacred cause.

For unionist and loyalists, a combination of the Battle of the Boyne, Scottish heritage and the Protestant faith contributed to a strong identification with the UK and its constitutional monarchy. Unionists, through political control, and loyalists, through sectarian violence, have fought for over a century to preserve the sovereignty of Northern Ireland. This brief historical summary makes it clear that the conditions for collective and transgenerational trauma were in place a long time before "The Troubles" started in 1969. A "burden of remembering" was passed along for over 100 years.

Today there are generations who were not alive during "The Troubles", or who are not aware of the peace process, and yet for them symbolic and structural memories of violent conflict remain. A history of civil violence remains in murals, memorials and peace walls:

> No one on either side of the peace line is allowed to forget history, at least the history of intercommunal murder. You pass it if you go out shopping or walking to school.[5]

In Northern Ireland, the historical tensions between different communities represent a powerful attachment to the past and its persuasive ideologies. A long-term attachment to the past is an unforgiving and heavy burden that distorts perceptions and shapes behaviours. Remembrance as a ritual and "remembering" as a human process can be emotional burdens passed on from one generation to the next, consciously or unconsciously. A practical example of trauma transmission is reflected in a speech delivered by a republican political activist in 2001. It was three years after the Belfast/Good Friday Agreement:

> Fellow republicans, I call upon you to educate our youth and instill in them a sense of pride in, and understanding of, the sacrifices of countless generations of men and women in the pursuit of Irish Freedom.[6]

Today, new generations with no lived experience of "The Troubles" are joining established paramilitary groups. This means individuals joining the New IRA or Real UVF are more likely to be trained by, or bond with, those with traumatic memories.

The legacy of the republican Bobby Sands is an illustration of the role of remembrance in the transmission of trauma. Great effort and energy have been expended by republicans and nationalists in the remembrance of Bobby Sand's time in prison, his hunger strike and subsequent death. Below is an extract from his diary as he started his hunger strike:

> I believe I am but another of those wretched Irishmen born of a risen generation with a deeply rooted and unquenchable desire for freedom.[7]

Bobby Sands was elected as an MP on 9 April 1981 and weeks later died a horrific death on 5 May. His political success was evidence of support from republican and nationalist communities in Northern Ireland but the republican stance on abstentionism, at the time, prevented him from sitting in a British Parliament or indeed the Stormont Government. Bobby Sand's memory has been respected at republican gatherings since his death. For some republicans his martyrdom continues to be a noble cause.

Remembrance can be a healthy expression of loss and an opportunity to reflect on the lessons that have been passed to us from our ancestors. The danger is that remembrance can entangle us in the past and cause us to revisit the memories and grievances that continue to haunt us. In Northern Ireland, rituals and ceremonies have become powerful political weapons that polarise communities and subvert the work of peacebuilding. The role of remembrance as a positive human ritual or a source of trauma bonding and transmission is an important strategic consideration for political leaders and community leaders alike:

> You can't expect people to be comfortable in a street where there is a memorial to a terrorist who would have killed them and may indeed have killed someone they knew and loved.[8]

What is transgenerational trauma?

Some families and communities in Northern Ireland continue to feel unsafe in their neighbourhoods despite the Belfast/Good Friday Agreement and this can be seen in the continued presence of "peace walls". Originally constructed in 1969 by British soldiers to protect Catholic communities from loyalist violence, they have become tourist attractions. To some local people, the walls are an essential security measure. However, these structures act as a constant reminder of the past and sustain the narrative of ongoing sectarian division and community conflict. The Northern Ireland Executive planned to start dismantling these walls by 2023. A combination of community resistance, the collapse of the devolved government and the commercial opportunities of a "tourist attraction" have stalled that plan.

The physical, psychological and behavioural effects of trauma can be transmitted from one generation to another in a number of ways:[9]

- Children of traumatised parents may be exposed to behaviours, emotional reactions and stressful family life.

- Survivors of war or conflict may manage their experience of trauma in the family unit in one of two ways: by staying silent or oversharing.
- Coping mechanisms employed to minimise the impact of trauma such as the use of alcohol or drugs can contribute to a deterioration in physical and mental health.

It is worth noting that language, symbols, rituals and physical structures such as "peace walls" all play a part in the transmission of trauma within families and across communities, and continue to pose a significant challenge for the development of sustainable peace.

"Troubles" related trauma and mental health

There is an abundance of academic research, government policy papers and publications from advocacy and community organisations which together confirm a link between "The Troubles" and poor mental health. The following section will briefly cover the major themes of transgenerational trauma and poor mental health emerging from academic research, policy development and the practical reality.

Reflections on academic research

It is clear that the traumatic experiences of a violent conflict have had a long-term effect on physical and mental health in Northern Ireland.[10] Even when the guns stopped and peacebuilding started, the possibility of transgenerational trauma remained. Current data on mental health in Northern Ireland indicates that several generations are presenting with the symptoms of anxiety, depression and PTSD.[11]

For example, the psychological impact of Bloody Sunday in 1972 extended to those wounded, those within range of gunfire, immediate family members of those killed or injured and a second generation who were not present at the time.[12] Research on transgenerational trauma confirms that post-conflict trauma symptoms can manifest as chronic health conditions such as anxiety, depression and PTSD.

The transgenerational effect can be seen in rising numbers of young people presenting with mental health issues or who have experienced self-harm and suicidal thoughts. A positive contribution to research was "Make Parity a Reality" in 2019 which urged a greater emphasis on mentally healthy communities and for people in leadership roles to have greater understanding or "lived experience" of mental health illness.[13]

Reflections on policy development

The "Bamford Review" published in 2009 represented an important step because it made a number of constructive recommendations to ensure positive mental health was taken seriously:[14]

- A reform of mental health legislation.
- A further shift from hospital to community-based services.
- The development of specialist services for children, young people and older people.
- Provision for those with addiction issues and those in the criminal justice system.
- The growth of a fully trained workforce to deliver mental health services.

This reflected a political recognition that a mental health crisis in Northern Ireland was a realistic possibility. Whether the recommendations factored in the link between conflict-related trauma and mental is unclear. The Bamford Review was however a positive step forward and was followed up with progress reviews and action plans. Two major themes appeared: an imperative to engage in a collaborative approach to developing services, and a transition from hospital to community-based provision. These recommendations proposed a transformation in the design of mental health services to a model that was more aligned to individual needs and flexible enough to provide for low- and high-intensity health conditions. This was an important change, especially in the light of research findings in the previous section on the transgenerational transmission of trauma.

An interesting development can be found in the "Strategy for the Development of Psychological Therapy Services" in 2010, which recommended the use of cognitive behavioural therapy (CBT) for initial assessment, diagnosis and early support.[15] This represented a significant change in the treatment for mild symptoms towards counselling and "talking therapies" and now with a greater focus on recovery and an individual's capacity to heal.

Policy documents from 2010 onwards continued to reflect a growing awareness that the symptoms of poor mental health are a highly individual experience which may or may not be linked to traumatic events but requires alternative forms of treatment to medication. Today CBT is used in mainstream mental health services for initial assessments, support and the treatment of low-intensity symptoms. The emergence of a customised "stepped" approach to care meant that mental health services could be designed to accommodate a range of individual needs from mild symptoms to severe or complex disorders.

A noticeable omission in government policy was the voices of the people who needed help with their mental health. This was addressed in 2011 with a review of health and social care called "Transforming Your Care"[16] based on public consultation and which acknowledged that both persistent levels of deprivation and the legacy of violent conflict were interconnected and contributed to poor mental health. Early intervention was seen as key to developing a mental health strategy and in 2014 "The Care Pathway" was introduced. This five-tier model is now used extensively for initial diagnosis and referrals to relevant care. The Care Pathway provided a more flexible approach with more services provided in the community. Below is an overview of the tiers:

Tier one: Self-directed help for mild stress and anxiety (problem-solving strategies)
Tier two: Primary care for mental health services (talking therapies)

Tier three: Specialist community mental health services (psychological therapies plus medication)
Tier four: Highly specialist conditions and complex needs (specific services involving a range of specialists)
Tier five: High-intensity mental health which affects quality of life (psychological therapies and medication). This might involve in-patient care.

In 2016, a major step forward took place as the Mental Health Capacity Act was introduced. The legislation represented a dramatic move away from involuntary based psychiatric treatment to a model that reflected dignity and respect. In the same year, Michelle O'Neill as Health Minister championed an initiative called "Delivering Together" which focused on a person-centred approach, early intervention and a more collaborative approach to service provision. It was publicised as a 10-year strategy but the collapse of the Northern Ireland Government between 2017 and 2020 brought progress on implementation to a halt. "Transforming Your Care" remains a key government policy.

Reflections from mental health professionals

Several interesting themes emerged from conversations with people working in mental health services and trauma healing from both NHS and private health care providers. Their practical experiences confirm that the legacy of violent conflict in Northern Ireland has impacted the mental health of several generations. The Mental Health Capacity Act in 2016 and the Care Pathway are regarded as positive, practical advances in addressing the diverse mental health needs across Northern Ireland.

Mental health professionals have serious concerns about a widening gap between demand for their services and the future funding that will be needed. The early detection of exposure to traumatic experiences or transgenerational trauma was seen as a critical aspect of mental health treatment. The use of psychological education and low-intensity approaches such as cognitive behavioural therapy (CBT) and counselling were recommended especially with individuals assessed as tier one or tier two in the Care Pathway. Currently, mental health professionals from all disciplines face a massive increase in demand for mental health services. There are larger numbers of younger age groups now seeking help that match the criteria for tier three and tier four where specialist care may be required. The waiting lists for treatment in tiers one and two are between nine and 12 months, which is frustrating for health professionals because the benefits of early treatment can be lost. The prevalence of medication for low-intensity mental health conditions is regarded as a missed opportunity to educate and empower people about their mental health.

Alignment of research, policy and practice

The alignment between academic research, government policy and "real world" practice is rarely neat or symmetrical. From the perspective of integrated health provision, insights gathered from the three perspectives of research, policy and practice indicate a partial alignment and some urgent practical dilemmas:

- Research and policy appear to coalesce around the need for collaboration in mental health service development and improved access to both hospital and community treatment. Professionals working with communities face complex challenges especially with an increased rate of self-harm and suicide rates in young people. The expansion of Family Support Hubs and introduction of trauma centres is an essential development in mental health provision.
- Extensive research into transgenerational trauma and the link with mental health aligns with practical challenges facing mental health professionals on the ground.
- The Care Pathway provides a model that helps to manage consistency in the provision of service, however it does not solve the urgent problem of supply and demand. Private providers of counselling and

therapy also report high demand but their services do not necessarily reach the people in most need of help.
- In reality poor mental health still carries a stigma and is seen as a lower priority to physical health. Education about the effects of trauma on the mind and body is currently taking place and this is deemed as an essential practice. Both research and policy publications champion a "person-centred approach" but the reality for health professionals is a significant shortfall in resources.

It appears that the "elephant in the room" is the current application of the tiered system of assessment. For low intensity conditions, such as chronic stress and anxiety, the choices are stark; a long wait, pay privately or accept a prescription. The Care Pathway has been successful as a diagnostic system, but the scale of resources needed has not been fully investigated, addressed or funded. Without a strong lead from the new Northern Ireland Executive and effective cross-party collaboration across the new Assembly, the implementation of mental health policies is in danger of stalling.

Sustainable peace and trauma healing

The response to a traumatic experience is highly individual and can be affected by the environment, context and age group. If we look closely, trauma conditions and the process of healing at an individual level are also mirrored in groups, communities and the wider society. Families and extended families can experience collective trauma, in which the "lived experience" of an individual family member may engulf a larger group of people in the original trauma. For sustainable peace to become a reality then a strategic, integrated approach to the provision of trauma healing needs to be in place supported by practical tools and guidance.

Academic research combined with substantive policy development spanning over a decade has not fully addressed the root causes of poor mental health in Northern Ireland. The transmission of trauma across generations is a sensitive issue and something of a political blind spot. The legacy of "The Troubles" remains and affects the health of individuals and families.

A practical way forward is to place a greater emphasis on a trauma-informed approach which involves a broader spectrum of other professionals e.g. social workers, teachers and the criminal justice system. Trauma-informed leadership is needed across different providers and community organisations because it is a constructive approach that supports transformational change and builds the societal capability needed for sustainable peace. In the future the work of trauma healing would not just be the responsibility of clinicians or therapists but a collaborative approach that educates and empowers family members, carers and friends.

An alternative perspective on forgiveness

Earlier in the chapter reference was made to acts of leadership that support sustainable peace and included apology, forgiveness and trust building. These acts are vital to conflict transformation and the promotion of good physical and mental health. Traumatic experiences impact mind and body and this has consequences for both physical and mental health. Over time individuals may develop coping strategies that mask the pain and hold off the memories. A trained professional can support recovery from a traumatic experience, but the individual does the real work.

This brings us back to the practice of forgiveness and one of humankind's biggest challenges after a violent conflict. Gordon Wilson was a devout Protestant Christian and this gave him the courage to reach out to both loyalist and republican paramilitaries. In the 1980s, in an environment of violent civil conflict, his approach to forgiveness was baffling to some Protestants.

Today, we know from neuroscience that an individual's nervous system copes with traumatic loss or shock in different ways. A trauma-informed leader recognises that the impact of violent conflict on the nervous system may be so strong that the idea of forgiveness is "unthinkable". The mind cannot process the enormity of the shocking event that has occurred. The problem with the idea of forgiveness is that it can become a dogma and bring an additional burden to a person already experiencing symptoms of trauma. However, a lack of forgiveness keeps people trapped in traumatic events and leaves them attached to the past and this is an important consideration for sustainable peace in Northern Ireland. The complexity is that the process of forgiving has no set structure or timing and over time, old grievances continue to impact physical and mental health.

The critical issue for political leaders is when people and their communities are living in fear, it is very difficult for them to grieve fully, forgive or make peace with the past. It would be foolish to underestimate the cultural and collective burden this represents to transformational change and any future vision of sustainable peace.

Characteristics of trauma-informed leaders

In Northern Ireland politicians are probably the most important group to become trauma-informed and to be more consciously aware of how their language, behaviours and actions impact their credibility as leaders. A positive development has been the cross-party collaboration and interest politicians have shown on mental health policy. However, this does not represent the scale and quality of the political will and leadership that will be needed to solve the growing mental health crisis in Northern Ireland. Trauma-informed leaders take a whole system view of change and engage collaboratively with others. They are recognisable by a high level of self-awareness of their motives, assumption and actions. Some notable characteristics trauma- informed leaders possess are:

An understanding of the transmission of trauma across generations

- A greater integration of trauma healing and conflict transformation initiatives.
- A greater appreciation that each new generation can inherit family trauma which if left unresolved can trap communities in historic grievances.
- A greater awareness of language and its role in the polarisation of, or connection between, communities and societies.

A commitment to weakening the links of transgenerational trauma

- Developing systems of remembering that honour ancestors and their legacies but which change the focus from painful memories to forgiveness, learning and change.
- Taking a strategic approach to healing trauma through collaborative leadership across schools, higher education, health and social services, churches and the custodial system.
- Focusing on a collaborative, partnership approach to trauma healing between different providers and approaches.
- Expanding the work of restorative justice, and forgiveness and reconciliation within and across communities.

Chapter summary: Trauma-informed leadership

This chapter has established the impact of traumatic experiences on poor mental health and provided evidence of transgenerational trauma within groups, families and communities in Northern Ireland. It is clear that academic research has had an impact on policy development and the provision of mental health services, but a collapsed government has meant that implementation and funding decisions have stalled.

This is a major blind spot for political leaders. While Northern Ireland has made great steps forward towards conflict transformation, the lack of decisive action to address trauma-related mental health issues is a major barrier to sustainable peace. There are generational consequences for people with lived experiences of "The Troubles" and now a new generation is exposed to the uncertainty following two decades of "stop-start" politics.

This chapter explored how an understanding of the impact of traumatic events on the mind and body can be an empowering experience. A personal realisation that everyone has their own specific way of dealing with threats to safety can help to counter the negative thoughts that bring toxic stress and anxiety e.g. blame, guilt and helplessness.

Through this exploration of trauma-informed leadership, it has become clear that the relationship between politicians and citizens needs a recalibration. Essential to transformation is recognition that past grievances, hatred towards specific individuals or groups, or political or religious dogma all deny our basic human needs for safety, dignity and social interaction. Political leaders have a responsibility to acknowledge the part they play in hindering the development of sustainable peace and engage fully with different agencies and charities working hard to raise awareness of trauma healing and poor mental health.

Chapter 5 will consolidate the insights from all the previous chapters and draw together learning about collaborative, transformational and trauma-informed leadership to make a strategic analysis of the form of political leadership needed in the future to facilitate sustainable peace.

Notes

1. Hartley, T. (1995) Forum for Peace and Reconciliation, Dublin Castle.
2. Cochrane, F. (2013) *Northern Ireland: The Reluctant Peace*, London, Yale University Press, p. 274.
3. Levine, P. (1997) *Waking the tiger: Healing Trauma: the innate capacity to transform overwhelming experiences,* Berkeley, CA, North Atlantic Books.

4. Diagnostic and Statistical Manual of Medical Disorders, *American Psychiatric Association,* September 2023. DSM criteria were first developed in the USA. British and European versions largely follow this model. Some clinicians disagree with DSM criteria and find them too rigid.
5. O'Doherty, M. (2023) *How to Fix Northern Ireland*, London, Atlantic Books, p. 28.
6. Price, M. (2001) *Irish Republican News,* p. 1. A republican activist affiliated with Republican Sinn Féin.
7. Sands, B. The Diary of Bobby Sands, *An Phoblacht,* 1 March 1981.
8. O'Doherty, M. (2023) *How to fix Northern Ireland*, London, Atlantic Books, p. 286.
9. Gough, M. (2017) *The Psychological Impact of "The Troubles" in Northern Ireland in Today's Children: A Post-Conflict, Transgenerational Perspective.* Queen's University, Belfast.
10. Troubled consequences: A report on the mental impact of the civil conflict in Northern Ireland, prepared for the Commission for Victims and Survivors, by Bamford Centre for Mental Health and Wellbeing, *University of Ulster,* published October 2011 at www.cvsni.org
11. Review of Mental Health statistics in Northern Ireland, *Office for Statistics Regulation,* 7 September 2021.
12. Miskelly, C. (2016) The Transgenerational Impact of "The Troubles" in Northern Ireland on the Family System, *Queen's University: Belfast,* pp. 28–29.
13. O'Neill, S., Heenan, D, & Betts, J. (2019) Making Parity a Reality: A Review of Mental Health Policies in Northern Ireland, *University of Ulster,* 21 June.
14. Dept. of Health. (2009). Bamford Review of Mental Health and Learning Disabilities <https://www.health-ni.gov.uk/articles/bamford-review-mentalhealth-and-learning disability>.
15. Dept. of Health. (2010). A Strategy for the Development of Psychological Therapy Service (June 2010) <https //www-health-ni.gov.uk/publications/strategy-development–psychological-therapy-service-2010>.
16. Dept. of Health (2011) Transforming your Care: A Review of Health and Social Care in Northern Ireland, www.dhsspsni.gov.uk

CHAPTER 5

Sustainable peace and political leadership

Reflections and insights

The previous chapter explored the transgenerational effect of trauma, the impact on physical and mental health across Northern Ireland and the consequences for sustainable peace. Evidence from current research, both academic and policy based, together with the views of mental health practitioners confirmed that "The Troubles" have had a transgenerational impact on the health of individuals, families and communities. Insights from an analysis of conflict-related trauma included current and ex-members of paramilitary organisations who have a role to play in creating sustainable peace.

Despite research and policy development on the links between mental health and post-conflict trauma, the current provision of mental health services remains underfunded and under-resourced. This represents a potential blind spot for political leaders who now face an irrefutable public health concern which could present a risk to sustainable peace in Northern Ireland. Early diagnosis of trauma-related mental health conditions can make a significant difference to the speed of recovery for an individual experiencing traumatic symptoms. For peace to be sustainable political leaders need to become more trauma-informed and acknowledge that a growing mental health crisis is one of the unseen human costs of "The Troubles".

This chapter will focus on political leadership and its role in both conflict transformation and the development of a robust political and social foundation for sustainable peace. The term "leaders" will encompass a wider body of people than elected politicians. It will include those in leadership roles working within a diverse range of third sector and civil society organisations e.g. charities, community development programmes and groups engaged in conflict transformation.

Reflections from previous chapters indicate that the goal of conflict transformation in Northern Ireland has been served well by collaborative leadership operating in cross-community initiatives and programmes. Ideally, this work is led by politicians but it does not necessarily start or end with them. With periods of collapsed government and an apparent lack of collective will to make power-sharing work, it is clear that elected politicians represent a significant barrier to the scale of collaboration needed to build sustainable peace. Consider the stark warning from Stephen McCarthy, MP (UUP), after his election success in October 2022: "We have squandered our peace".[1]

A future vision of sustainable peace is a possibility but it requires a significant transformation in the way politics is conducted and a constructive healthy challenge to a traditional, top-down view of political leadership. In previous chapters, new forms of leadership were examined to discover practical insights into conflict transformation and how to create a society with the will and resilience to stay at peace. The purpose of this chapter is to consolidate the insights from previous chapters and clarify the conditions needed for sustainable peace, and the quality of political leadership needed to make this happen.

Has the peace been squandered?

Stephen McCarthy's remark brings an interesting challenge for Members of the Legislative Assembly (MLAs) and ministers in the Executive. If the peace has been squandered then the responsibility lies with those in positions of power and their ability to manage the duality of their political affiliations with their collective accountability to the people of Northern Ireland. If we reflect on the forms of leadership discussed in previous chapters, it was clear that there have been leaders in government and civil society with the insight and tenacity to keep the momentum of peace moving forward. Five major themes on leadership have emerged:

- Acts of leadership
- The contribution of women leaders
- Conflict transformation and leadership
- Contemporary forms of leadership
- A new paradigm for political leadership

Acts of leadership

Acts of leadership can bring momentum to initiating and building peace. Some acts of leadership emerge from unexpected places and are not necessarily carried out by those with power and authority. To fully appreciate this phenomenon it is important to differentiate between the role of a leader and acts of leadership. A leadership role acts as a container that confers identity, legitimacy and power on the role holder. Individuals bring their own unique style and motivation to their leadership role and this observable as behaviours and actions.

In practice, leadership is a natural human response to situations and a manifestation of the individual's personal power and values. Influential leadership is not necessarily a factor of status, authority or power. In previous chapters, there were examples of acts of leadership from the 1970s to the present day that served peace building and were a testimony to human resilience in the face of crisis, violence and loss. Many of these examples of leadership demonstrated that people felt driven to act, to serve and help others. The question of whether they had the authority or power to act was clearly a secondary priority to them.

The contribution of women leaders

The role of women in peacebuilding has emerged as an important consideration for the future. Since the 1970s women acting as individuals or part of a larger group have demonstrated their ability to unite communities in the cause of peace. During the negotiations for the Belfast/ Good Friday Agreement in 1998, the Northern Ireland Women's Coalition (NIWC) had two places at the negotiating table. The recommendations from this anti-sectarian political party included: initiatives for young people, mixed housing, integrated education and the creation of Civic Forums. These initiatives were cross-community, collaborative and addressed the issue of sustainable peace as early as 1998. However, if we compare this progress with contemporary research, a picture emerges that confirms that peace is at risk of being squandered:

> Women's participation in public life was formally included as a provision in the peace agreement and while there has been some notable success for women, it is not possible to say that full and equal participation in public life has been secured.[2]

In 1998, the presence of the NIWC leaders helped to ground peace negotiations because their leaders modelled behaviours that were more collaborative and less combative. Despite this positive contribution to the Belfast/Good Friday Agreement, the NIWC struggled to gain electoral support in a political climate that reflected polarised political divisions. The party disbanded in 2006.

Northern Ireland has an enduring and vocal civic culture, which is manifested as political challenges from grassroots through organisations such as charities and community groups. Women leaders continue to be influential leaders in their communities, powerful advocates for peace and represent a crucial component for the checks and balances that ensure best practice governance. They have been less successful at challenging and changing the traditional political divisions.

Conflict transformation and leadership

> Rather than a moment of radical change, transformation follows from the cumulative impact of symbolic gesture, specific legal provision, procedural practice, mechanisms of accountability, and an engaged and vibrant civil society.[3]

Conflict transformation requires political cooperation between leaders in government, local government and across a diverse range of civil society organisations. In previous chapters transformational and collaborative leadership were illustrated through the various attempts at peacebuilding between 1969 and 1998. These forms of leadership challenged the status quo and started to create a common ground between conflicting parties that would over time support peace talks.

There is an enlightening leadership story about Mo Mowlam, MP, who was appointed by Prime Minister Tony Blair to be Secretary of State for Northern Ireland in 1997 with a remit to progress the peace talks. Her leadership style enabled her to connect with diverse groups and to influence negotiating teams to stay grounded in the "real world". In January 1998, Mo Mowlam visited loyalist paramilitaries in prison to persuade them to maintain their ceasefire and help to keep the peace talks moving forward. She did not consult the British Prime Minister or his Chief of Staff and at the same time risked the fury of unionist politicians:

> She didn't think of consulting us and went straight ahead and announced she was going to the Maze to meet UDA prisoners. We didn't approve and if she had asked us we would certainly have said no.[4]

Mo Mowlam used a transformational approach to her relationship with paramilitaries and earned the respect of both republicans and loyalist groups. She appreciated that a sustainable peace could only be achieved if paramilitary groups were consulted, however heinous their crimes might appear to other stakeholders. Mo Mowlam's act of leadership is a political lesson in conflict transformation and reflects a hidden danger for sustainable peace when "talking to the enemy" is regarded as abhorrent. This aspect of peacebuilding is covered in more detail in Chapter 1 with a short case study of Margaret Thatcher's command and control style of leadership and her relationship with republican paramilitaries.

Contemporary forms of leadership

In the first three chapters a historical approach was adopted to reveal the leadership values and behaviours that contribute to conflict resolution and to differentiate those from the acts of leadership that escalate conflict. In Chapter 4 the focus turned to trauma-informed leadership, a contemporary response to the intergenerational impact of "The Troubles" on public health and a current risk to sustainable peace. The traumatic impact of conflict on physical and mental health does not respect class, political affiliation, status or power and can manifest as undiagnosed symptoms.

In terms of sustainable peace, trauma-informed leadership has a major role to play in understanding why sectarian attitudes and behaviours continue to shape the culture of Northern Ireland. When insecurity remains part of people's lives, the experience of not feeling safe is transmitted from one generation to the next. Sectarianism is symptomatic of several decades of traumatic responses to direct and indirect violence.

The fact that sectarian attacks continue and "peace walls" remain is an important signifier of ongoing threat, whether experienced or perceived, in some communities. Each attack, whether verbal or violent, squanders a little more of the hard-earned peace. There is an opportunity for political leaders to implement a more systematic, cross-party response to this contemporary public health challenge and minimise the risk to sustainable peace.

A new paradigm for political leadership

Conflict transformation is served by peace agreements which contain structural and systematic political reforms but the quality of political leadership in the aftermath of conflict is critical to trust building, constructive relationships and the timely implementation of agreed reforms. Current political leaders have inherited the positive aspects of the Belfast/Good Friday Agreement, but they have also drifted away from the principles behind power sharing and regressed to old political habits to conduct government business.

The final peace agreement had a number of unintended consequences including radical opposition from both republican and loyalist paramilitary groups. In the time period between 1998 and the early 2020s paramilitary groups, both republican and loyalist, have continued to operate along old enemy lines albeit with new branding e.g. "New IRA" and "Real UVF". Today their presence represents a critical issue for sustainable peace in Northern Ireland and one which requires collaborative political work and cross-community engagement to resolve.

Reasonable political objections, from both republicans and unionists, to the terms of the Belfast/Good Friday Agreement have become entangled with sectarian division and a shared legacy of violence. The intention of "constructive ambiguity" was to bring an end to violence and facilitate an agreement that key stakeholders could sign up to. The irony of "constructive ambiguity" was that it created fertile ground for enduring polarised political and religious views.

The consequences of division and polarisation were palpable in the aftermath of the peace agreement when decommissioning became a new battleground but now between republican and unionist politicians. Today political leadership in Northern Ireland remains polarised and continues to be shaped by the past despite the influence of moderate political parties such as the SDLP and the Alliance Party. The structural reforms designed to bring a more equitable model of power sharing have created a political culture in which the dominant parties, Sinn Féin and the DUP, have the power to collapse the Northern Ireland Government.

Conflict transformation and sustainable peace are intergenerational processes that require patience, trust building and a radical change in leadership behaviours. Elected politicians have the role and political remit to lead social and political change. It is clear that leadership behaviours which model political collaboration are more likely to foster trust than displays of polarised attitudes and language:

> They were brought to agreement in order to end violent conflict that had lasted decades, through a peace process, and then instead of putting division behind them they have institutionalised it.[5]

Current political rhetoric conveys the importance of transformation and change for Northern Ireland, but the reality is a political vacuum created by leaders who appear to be unaware that the political and societal transformation starts with them and their moral compasses. On a positive note, the voices of civil society remain a strong, inventive and constructive political force to challenge the behaviours of elected politicians.

What are the core conditions for "positive peace"?

In this section positive peace in Northern Ireland will be discussed to illustrate how the achievement of positive peace can act as a precursor to sustainable peace. Three core themes will be explored:

- Relationships, structures and policy
- Co-production of government policy
- Political leadership and mission drift

Relationships, structures and policy

Peacemaking and peacebuilding are processes in which antagonists learn to trust each other enough to create new structures, but more importantly to adopt new attitudes and navigate workable relationships. In previous chapters, the collaborative leadership potential of the roles of First Minister and deputy First Minister was illustrated through the relationship between Ian Paisley and Martin McGuinness in 2007. As the first role holders both political leaders found a way to share power and make their political remit workable.

It is fascinating to note that, back in 2007, Ian Paisley and Martin McGuinness both made a conscious choice to make the power-sharing model work for the interests of peace in Northern Ireland. While their individual personalities and differences surfaced in private, they presented a united front. Both men provided a powerful lesson that a collaborative leadership approach can circumvent a less than perfect structure. Models of governance are rarely perfect theoretical structures but they draw intense intellectual debate especially when they appear to be failing. Inevitably the response is to restructure, rewrite the strategy, create a new policy or call for a review. A good example can be observed in the responses of unionist politicians to a Sinn Féin electoral majority in 2022. DUP politicians led a challenge calling for a review of the power-sharing model and a redefinition of the consent principle.

The structures of power-sharing represent only one dimension of change needed for positive and sustainable peace and it is for political leaders to make a conscious choice to invest in their cross-party relationships. A practical example can be observed in the political process of policy making. In Northern Ireland there are cross-party initiatives producing well researched and well crafted policies with sound recommendations. However, the evidence for consistent and practical implementation is less convincing, especially for the people working on the ground who serve the needs of communities.

In the public domain politicians generate detailed policy implementation plans, progress reviews and action plans. These documents are efficient structural responses to social change and conflict transformation, but they risk becoming meaningless political activities with little substantive evidence of action and change. In contrast, leaders in third sector and civil society organisations are closer to real world issues and more likely to be vocal on the quality of government decisions and evidence of practical actions.

It is interesting to compare the political rhetoric from a government policy document on community development, "To develop more cohesive and engaged communities"[6] with the voices of people working on the "Thirty Project", an initiative funded by the Holywell Trust:

> I think we are fed up with not having a voice. I think the polarisation of thought has totally cut off the majority of regular people that need to have a voice.[7]

This remark represents the tip of the iceberg for many people operating within community development programmes and working to compensate for the political vacuum left by a collapsed government. The risk to sustainable peace lies in a widening gap between an experienced third sector/civil society closer to the heart of change and an elected government unable to function effectively.

A collapsed government is limited in the extent and scope of financial and political decision making and this has been a contributing factor to an expansion of the third sector in Northern Ireland. A plethora of grassroots organisations, charities, philanthropic ventures and community programmes have developed to provide vital services and support. Funding and resourcing remain perpetual challenges for many of these organisations but their continued existence signifies the scale of need across communities and the determination of the people to provide the services that are so very needed.

Many of these organisations deliver services that have an immediate and practical contribution to creating the conditions for sustainable peace. Each has their own mission, strategy and governance with operational models largely shaped by the amount and source of funding. A crucial political consideration for the future of sustainable peace will be to address the roles, potential vulnerability and fragmentation of the third sector.

Co-production of government policy

The informal political power of civil society in Northern Ireland has been a crucial driver for positive peace and comprises a diverse spectrum of organisations with vital knowledge about the needs of families and communities and the issues they face. As a result the style of leadership in these organisations is generally more flexible and creative than their government counterparts they are better equipped to inform policy decisions and strategic plans. Co-produced political and social policy between a formal government and an informal civil society is a practical solution but it requires a radical change in political leadership from a traditional "top-down" approach to one of co-production. The transformation from "top-down" leadership to power- sharing as necessary in the co-production of services requires a radical change in leadership behaviours. A primary issue is the state of leadership readiness of both elected politicians and civil society leaders to re-calibrate the relationship between government and citizens.

A worked example in Northern Ireland can be seen in the civic forums introduced in 2002 as part of the Belfast/Good Friday Agreement and mothballed two years later. In 2020, a new government policy announced a greater commitment to civil engagement and the reintroduction of civic forums.[8] The policy was shelved as the result of another collapse of the Northern Ireland Government but there remains a strong case for the return of civic forums as a source of practical ideas to feed into government policy:

> Local people need to be trusted on some of the more difficult issues that we have. If people are given the information and the opportunity to discuss them, they'll arrive at positive solutions.[9]

Civic forums represent an opportunity for elected politicians to tap into practical solutions that have already passed a reality check and have the support of local people. This takes party political alliances out of the equation and relieves politicians of any conflict of interest they may face. All political stakeholders gain from a reassurance that any form of civil engagement and empowerment represents good governance and a practical step towards sustainable peace.

Political leadership and mission drift

A major challenge for sustainable peace in Northern Ireland is the scale of different political interests with elected politicians, local government leaders, civil servants and civil society leaders all working in the same space. It is a cluttered arena made more complex by the "stop/start" periods of direct rule from Westminster when the devolved Northern Ireland Government loses the opportunity to turn policy into practical action.

While elected representatives are marking time and, controversially, taking a salary, community programmes, projects and charities all continue to function. These organisations, their leaders and staff do not pause when there is a collapsed government. On the contrary, third sector activity is expanding further to meet the needs of communities and currently there is a growth in private sector alliances and philanthropic ventures.

A rapidly expanding third sector does, however, carry the risk of mission drift and this is related to the way organisations are funded. For example, charities operating independently are especially vulnerable to mission drift because of their reliance on donations and many have conflicting demands from service users, trustees, donors and statutory bodies. This comment is a typical early signal of mission drift for a small charity:

> Community workers can't take any more. I am doing peacebuilding, food banks and people are coming in and talking to me about their mental health.[10]

Some charities and community groups form alliances with philanthropic organisations and for them funding challenges recede but different threats to stability can emerge e.g. conflicts over strategic direction and leadership control. Charities and community groups may have strong founder values and missions but funding can drive leadership behaviours and how the organisation operates, e.g. if funding is linked to a specific community then the opportunity for cross-community initiatives may become less of a priority.

In 2013, a Department of Social Development review on tackling disadvantage and building sustainable communities concluded that there were too many programmes and too many governance structures in the existing organisations.[11] This was seen as overlapping roles in service delivery and competition for funding. Bids for funding are not necessarily value driven or serve the needs of a community, and in practice it can come down to being skilful at writing bids.

Mission drift can occur in organisations partnered with large institutions such as the National Health Service. Counselling is a good example and frequently involves a charity or private sector organisation delivering specific services that are linked to mainstream health provision. The providing organisation will be commissioned and the service provision subject to Care Quality Commission (CQC) inspection. Mission drift in these organisations is experienced daily because the funding model brings a conflict of interests between contract compliance and compassion for client needs.

In Northern Ireland, the quality of third sector activity is a major driver for positive and sustainable peace. However, it is not necessarily well coordinated, funded equitably or services distributed fairly to communities in most need. There is a risk that third sector activity becomes so cluttered and fragmented it loses direction and this is why the relationship between government and civil society has to be more collaborative and act as a societal compass for sustainable peace.

In this section three major themes have been identified to illustrate the current position regarding positive peace in Northern Ireland. All themes reflect the need for a balance between policy, strategy and action and this can be achieved by collaboration across the elected government, civil society and third sector organisations:

- The need to develop a political paradigm in which quality relationships drive a shared mission of sustainable peace and balance the inevitable conflict between polarised political interests.
- The development of co-production methods to generate policies that balance long-term vision with pressing operational issues in health/ social care, housing and education.
- The need to consolidate and build on the achievements of the third sector and to balance their value-led missions with funding strategies which promote collaboration.

How do we know whether a positive peace is becoming sustainable?

The signs of sustainable peace can be observed when the root causes of the original conflict have either been addressed through political and social reform or there is political commitment and transparent funding decisions to remove the hidden inequities that remain. A crucial sign can be observed in the behaviour of elected politicians and how they balance their political allegiances with cross-party collaboration.

In the aftermath of a violent conflict there are some key priorities that need to be addressed in order to begin the journey to sustainable peace.

The following headings will be used to review where Northern Ireland is in terms of sustainable peace and what the political priorities might be at the time of going to print:[12]

- *Political perspective* and the need for stable government, new power structures and efforts to re-calibrate relationships.
- *Military transitions* and the need for investment in ongoing peace initiatives to prevent a recurrence of violence e.g. re-entry of combatants into civilian life.
- *Community security* and the creation of a sense of physical and psychological safety especially with respect to human rights.
- *Community engagement and empowerment* and the development of resources, capacity and capability across civil society to systematically transform the root causes of the original conflict.
- *Community health and wellbeing* and the equitable funding and provision of physical and mental health services, social care and housing.

Political perspective

> Northern Ireland needs institutions that have the resilience to withstand political disagreement without collapse.[13]

A sound political structure in conjunction with collaborative behaviours between political leaders is essential for sustainable peace. The relationships built during peace negotiations and final treaty ratification, however fragile, will need reinforcement and development. The Belfast/Good Friday Agreement was promoted as a blueprint for conflict transformation and addressed a full spectrum of political commitments including human rights, social and political reform, and the development of civil society as champions of peace and change.

A major consideration for sustainable peace is the quality and transparency in how political leaders make decisions. The trust between government and citizens is damaged if dominant political parties are seen to control the distribution of power and resources. In Northern Ireland "consensus models" have been developed to distribute European peace funds across communities in Northern Ireland. To achieve this, key stakeholders, e.g. politicians, businesses, central government officials and community organisations, work together and agree a set of principles. The introduction of decision making principles ensures that challenging discussions and decisions are based on transparent and quantifiable outcomes.[14] This is an example of "power-sharing" at its best.

However, the formal structures of power-sharing in the Northern Ireland Government established in 1998 have become a "game of collapse" between the two dominant political parties. Both Sinn Féin and the DUP have been instrumental in delaying vital political decisions and taking turns to collapse the devolved government. Sustainable peace can only become a viable aspiration if both Ministers and MLAs are trusted to serve the best interests of all. Today this is not the case in Northern Ireland with many citizens exasperated with the behaviour of politicians. These remarks from Jonathan Tonge, academic and political commentator, illuminate a major political barrier to sustainable peace:

> I would give the Good Friday Agreement a nine out of ten as a peace deal – if you look at the death toll before and after the agreement there has been dramatic progress. In terms of a political deal however, I would give it five out of ten because political instability has been the norm.[15]

Military transitions

With the signing of the Belfast/Good Friday Agreement in 1998 the scene was set for conflict resolution and conflict transformation rather than sustainable peace. The immediate challenge was to persuade the paramilitary organisations to end violence.

In theory ceasefires, the disarming of combatants and the decommissioning of weapons has both practical and symbolic goals: to stop the violence, prevent it reoccurring and signal a peace process. In Northern Ireland the political work of resolving the scope, timings and nature of disarmament and decommissioning was arduous but republican and unionist politicians did reach agreement. The provisional IRA effectively put themselves into retirement in 2005 and loyalist paramilitaries followed in 2007.

A key inhibitor of sustainable peace was the manner in which the combatants on both sides were demobilised. Overnight this represented a seismic change in identity and political purpose for both republican and loyalist paramilitaries. Both sides had been engaged in an extended civil conflict in a relatively small geographical area and were now expected to adapt and carry on as normal in their communities. At the time, the resettlement and reintegration of paramilitary veterans was not high on the political agenda.

It is important to acknowledge that back in the 1970s republican military volunteers were fighting for a united Ireland and loyalist volunteers were fighting republicans to preserve the union. Both parties believed they had a legitimate reason to engage in physical violence. This legacy remains for a small minority but it would be foolish to minimise their influence on sustainable peace. The New IRA's 2024 New Year message is interesting in its content and tone:

> The IRA today reiterates its fight for Irish independence, in all the forms it might take. We have shown in the past 12 months that we still have the volunteers and the capability to target members of the crown forces where and when we see fit; we will continue to do so.[16]

This is a cold, chilling message and quite different from traditional republican warrior talk which focuses on commemorating fallen heroes. The message is interesting because it dignifies the mission of the New IRA and distances them from criminal behaviour in Northern Ireland. The existence of armed paramilitaries, both republican and loyalist, and their current operations in Northern Ireland represents a substantial threat to sustainable peace. Their outreach to younger generations is a disturbing social trend that brings echoes of "The Troubles" back into communities and incites sectarian behaviour, language and even violence.

Community security and a sense of safety

Direct and indirect violence continues in Northern Ireland from both loyalist and republican paramilitaries and includes a full spectrum of criminal activity, punishment beatings, kneecappings and intimidation. Acts of violence are now less about the sovereignty of Northern Ireland and more about past sectarian grievances:

> It's a cold peace. It hasn't involved society reintegrating which means the divisions that caused the conflict are still there.[17]

Ongoing sectarian division is felt by young people who get caught up in acts of violence and entangled in their parents' and grandparents' experiences of sectarianism. "Taig" (Catholic) and "Prod" (Protestant) continue to remain derogatory terms to label and intimidate. A recent example of the menace of these terms and the violent consequences was shared in the Introduction to this book.

The inclusion of paramilitary members and veterans in future politics may be unpalatable but, without them, peace is at risk from small groups engaged in their "unfinished business". An interesting approach to the problem is being championed by organisations such as the Social Change Initiative, a community-based restorative justice organisation working with loyalists. A philosophical and cultural transformation from punitive to restorative justice is being tested but is not mainstream as yet, and is regarded cynically by some.

A political advocate of restorative justice is Naomi Long, leader of the Alliance Party, who has the experience of several periods of duty as Justice Minister. In 2023, with her influence, a collaborative approach towards policy on restorative justice was launched which included redress for victims of low-level crime and opportunities for reintegrating former combatants.[18]

Community empowerment and engagement

Earlier in the chapter it was concluded that conflict transformation relies on the decisions and motivations of political leaders willing to address the root causes of the original conflict. Different political stakeholders may have different perspectives on the root causes and this is why sustainable community development is key to building a realistic picture of the needs of different communities in Northern Ireland. The current lack of civic forums is a concern because it was a specific stipulation of the Belfast/Good Friday Agreement:

> There is no structure for citizens to feed into government policy. We feel as though local people need to be trusted on some of the more difficult issues that we have.[19]

In the absence of the reintroduction of civic forums new projects have emerged which focus on practical solutions e.g. the Civic Initiative, a project aimed at the "advancement of peace, reconciliation and wellbeing in Northern Ireland".[20] In addition, there are community organisations specifically focused on empowering women, developing their leadership and building their confidence to enter politics.[21] There are groups working with young people, ex-paramilitaries and minorities all of whom have a legitimate voice and place in contributing to sustainable peace. All these initiatives demonstrate the resilience and dedication of the grassroots in Northern Ireland to continue the work of building peace:

> The most hopeful transformative message lies in the experience of Northern Ireland's civil society, which has played a significant role in securing elements of the Agreement and which, since 1998, has impressively advocated the transformative potential of the Agreement with no end-date on its work.[22]

Community health and wellbeing

In 2016 an ambitious 10-year government plan was launched called "Health and Wellbeing 2026: Delivering Together". The focus on health and social care had traditionally been planned and managed around structures, buildings and specialist services. The long-term costs of this model are not sustainable. A combination of public consultation and expert knowledge concluded that the strategic focus needed to change to patients' needs and service users' voices. Where possible this would be delivered in the community with specialist services available when needed.

"Delivering Together" identified the need for reform in health and social care and recommended practical strategies to ensure sustainability. It was a comprehensive document and a road map for transformational change in Northern Ireland. Michelle O'Neill, Minister of Health, communicated some interesting rhetoric at the time, but within the year, the Executive had collapsed again:

> We are determined to move beyond short-term approaches and crisis management. This Executive is united as never before in its commitment to take the right, perhaps difficult decisions.[23]

The proposed reforms to service delivery, early diagnosis and preventative strategies were aligned with new models of designing and organising care provision and included innovative suggestions for leadership and staff development, co-production and collaboration across disciplines. Between January 2017 and January 2020 the devolved government was collapsed and "Delivering Together" effectively stalled with valuable time, funds and effort squandered. An opportunity to ground sustainable peace by transforming health and social care was also squandered.

A new paradigm for political leadership

In January 2020 the British and Irish Governments worked together to find a way to restore the devolved Northern Ireland Government to a more permanent basis capable of implementing policies such as "Delivering Together". It was called the "New Decade, New Approach" and it set out priorities for the Executive and clear principles for the conduct of both the Executive and Assembly:

> The parties have therefore agreed to an ambitious package of measures to strengthen transparency and governance arrangements in the Assembly and Executive in line with international best practice.[24]

The purpose of the document was to encourage the devolved government of Northern Ireland to reconvene, work more productively and devise protocols on how to conduct business. A review of "New Decade, New Approach" in the context of sustainable peace could be seen as a significant indictment of the behaviours of political leaders. The document, which was referred to as a "deal" spelt out the form of leadership and accountability expected of an effective government. It also presented a list of urgent priorities with a primary concern being health and social care. The tone and content of the document wiped out any pretence of an effective body of politicians working in the best interests of Northern Ireland.

Earlier in the section, a series of conditions for sustainable peace were outlined: *political, military, community safety, community engagement* and *health*. Sustainable peace is dependent on the congruence between these conditions and the quality of strategic leadership at government level.

Throughout this chapter, it has become clear that within civil society and third sector organisations there are collaborative and transformational leaders and staff who are committed to peace in Northern Ireland. There are examples of community development, empowerment and transformational projects that actively facilitate sustainable peace. All their efforts help to prevent a "conflict trap" and a drift back to violence. The strategic capability in these organisations although developed in a smaller context represents vital resources for politicians.

The arena of health and social care reforms will require significant government support and funding. The implementation of these reforms has been comprehensively researched and they represent a positive way forward for Northern Ireland. The responsibility rests squarely on the shoulders of elected politicians. The reform of health and social care will require collaborative cross-party leadership from both the Executive and the Assembly and a clear focus on the best interests of all the people. The current quality of physical and mental health in Northern Ireland is a major challenge to sustainable peace and political progress in this field would actively and publicly address the root causes of the original conflict.

The political "weak link" in terms of sustainable peace is not primarily the structure of power-sharing but the behaviour of a minority of political leaders who do not possess the vision or will to see beyond a polarised view of Northern Ireland's future.

Chapter summary

Radical change is a difficult process and requires committed political leadership and a clear unambiguous strategy. The transformation of Northern Ireland has been served well by individual acts of leadership that nudged the peace process along or demonstrated a novel way of resolving issues. The development of a sustainable peace will require patience and a holistic, integrated approach from the devolved government. Structural and systems changes may appear to be an obvious starting point because they are easier to measure but cultural and behavioural changes are key to making peace sustainable. Ironically, cultural and behavioural changes are less visible and lose the attention of political leaders especially close to elections.

The hidden costs of "The Troubles" include poor mental and physical health and continued deprivation in parts of Northern Ireland. While the original causes of the conflict have not been fully addressed, a range of policies published in the past five years indicate the politicians are aware but not necessarily collaborative enough to push on with tough decisions. There is however a greater awareness of the transgenerational impact of conflict on health and the practical resources needed to help people heal themselves.

The partial success of the Belfast/Good Friday Agreement has left some communities feeling unsafe. Security is valued as a human right for citizens of a post-conflict society and a major political priority will be further development of a "joined up" strategy to prevent a recurrence of violence. Paramilitaries continue to have control in some communities in Northern Ireland. A recurrence of violence triggered in a post-conflict society is generally due to an economic or political reason continuing to exist. This is particularly relevant to extended civil conflicts such as that in Northern Ireland where partition, sectarian divisions and religious differences have created a complex legacy for political leaders.

A new paradigm for political leadership will be manifested in Northern Ireland when politicians acknowledge the complexity of a modern post-conflict society and learn to collaborate on substantive social and political issues.

Notes

1. Stephen McCarthy, @smcarthynire, Twitter, 15 August 2022, <https://twitter.com/smccarthynire/status/1559276305669020892>.
2. The Belfast Good Friday Agreement and transformative change: promise, power and solidarity. Israel Law Review (2023), 1–33. doi: 10.1017/S0021223723000031 Cambridge University Press, p. 11.
3. The Belfast Good Friday Agreement and transformative change: promise, power and solidarity. Israel Law Review (2023), 1–33 doi: 10.1017/S0021223723000031 Cambridge University Press, p. 2.
4. Powell, J. (2008) Great Hatred: Little Room: Making Peace in Northern Ireland, Bodley Head, London, p. 28.
5. O'Doherty, M. (2023) *How to Fix Northern Ireland*, Atlantic Books, London, p. 291.
6. Urban Regeneration and Community Development Policy Framework, Department of Social Development, July 2023, p. iii.
7. Antoinette Morrow, quoted in Simpson, C. (2023) *Good Friday Agreement: 'We're fed up with not having a voice',* the detail, 27 April, p. 1.
8. *New Decade, New Approach*, 9 January 2020. <https://assets.publishing.service.gov.uk>.
9. Deane, G. (2023) quoted in the Good Friday Agreement: 'We're fed up with not having a voice', *the detail* 27 April, p. 1.
10. Weir, E. (2023) Shankill Women's Centre, *the detail* 27 April.
11. Urban Regeneration and Community Development Policy Framework, Department of Social Development, July 2023, p. 21.
12. Walter, B, F. (2011) Conflict R and the Sustainability of Peace, *World Bank.*
13. Effectiveness of Belfast/Good Friday Institutions, Pivotal Public Policy Forum, 13 January 2023.

14. PEACEPLUS PROGRAMME 2021–2027, Special EU Programmes Body, <https://www.seupb.eu>.
15. Tonge, J. (2023) quoted in The guns are gone but the sectarian divide is as strong as ever, *The Times*, 8 April, p. 32.
16. New IRA Statement, paper copies appeared on walls in Dublin and it was reported in *Irish Republican News*, 4 January 2024.
17. Tonge, J. (2023) quoted in "The guns are gone but the sectarian divide is as strong as ever", *Sunday Times*, 8 April, p. 32.
18. Draft Protocol on Restorative Justice launched by Naomi Long, 27 February 2023, <www.justice-ni.gov.uk>.
19. Gerald Deane, Director of the Holywell Trust, quoted from *the detail*, 27 April 2023.
20. Civic Initiative (@CivicInitNI)/X founded 2023.
21. A project called "Change makers" is organised by the Shankill Women's Centre, <https://www.shamkillwomenscentre.org.uk>.
22. The Belfast Good Friday Agreement and transformative change: promise, power and solidarity. Israel Law Review (2023), 1–33. doi: 10.1017/S0021223723000031 Cambridge University Press, p. 1.
23. Health and Wellbeing 2026: Delivering Together, Department of Health, www.org-nigov.uk, p. 3.
24. New Decade, New Approach, 2020, <https://assets.publishingservice.gov.uk>.

Postscript

Political implications of Brexit

Political events in Northern Ireland have moved rapidly towards a return to the devolved power-sharing government. The impact of the UK leaving the European Union (EU) in 2020 meant that trade between the UK, Northern Ireland and the Irish Republic (EU) became more complex. The British Government and the EU set out post-Brexit trade conditions in the "Northern Ireland Protocol". This agreement was published in January 2021 and included border checks, a politically sensitive subject and adamantly rejected by the DUP party. Their politicians walked out of Stormont in February 2022 causing the collapse of the power-sharing government.

A second agreement, the "Windsor Framework" in 2023 simplified trade conditions by introducing a two-lane system to speed up goods arriving in Northern Ireland from the UK. The DUP also rejected this agreement on the grounds that a trading border threatened the existence of the union between Northern Ireland and the UK.

The Independent Reporting Commission (IRC) in December 2023 neatly summarised one of the current leadership challenges facing political leaders and identified a crucial barrier to sustainable peace. The IRC report recommended the need for a new paradigm of political leadership behaviours and new forms of cross-party collaboration more likely to serve the best interests of the people of Northern Ireland.

30 January 2024: Safeguarding the Union

The requirement for customs checks for goods from the UK to Northern Ireland have been dropped in the latest attempt to persuade the DUP to return to government. The paper was called "Safeguarding the Union" and is an interesting document which focuses on safeguarding the union and protecting the internal UK market. In January 2024 Jeffrey Donaldson as leader of the DUP confirmed that the party would end their two-year boycott of the devolved Northern Ireland Government.

The new Stormont Government faces pressing operational challenges ranging from a public health crisis, workers' strikes and the continued presence of paramilitaries. The credibility of political leadership in Northern Ireland is in plain sight of the world and this is not the time for a return to historical grievances and political games. Naomi Long, leader of the Alliance Party and Minister for Justice, summed up a major issue for the new government:

> What is clear is the fragility of relationships, not just between parties but also inside some parties. They simply cannot withstand another collapse.[1]

3 February 2024: "A moment of profound significance"

Twenty months after the General Election of 2022 Michelle O'Neill, a republican, was confirmed as First Minister of Northern Ireland. The immediate response from the Sinn Féin president, Mary Lou McDonald, based in Dublin, was constructive, strategic and with no mention of Irish unity:

> Sinn Féin will now engage with all parties and both governments to ensure we all now press on without delay. It is vital that there is political stability to address the scale of crisis across our public services.[2]

The political rhetoric from the new First Minister, Michelle O'Neill, is also interesting because it brings the focus back to Northern Ireland and the peace process. Her words avoid sovereignty issues and the possibility of Irish unity. Below is a short extract from a longer speech that demonstrates a transformational and collaborative approach to leadership and a smart grip on the moral ground:

> I am wholeheartedly committed to continuing the work of reconciliation between all our people. None of us are being asked or expected to surrender who we are. Our allegiances are equally legitimate. My eyes are firmly fixed on the future. On unifying people and society.[3]

The political rhetoric communicates a republican focus on the immediate social issues facing the people of Northern Ireland with no reference to the sovereignty issues that are historical and divisive. The challenges for republican leaders will be to manage the expectations of nationalist and republican supporters of a united Ireland and resist the temptation to embroil themselves in old battles with the DUP.

A new political partnership "We are born equal"[4]

First Minister, Michelle O'Neill (Sinn Féin) and deputy First Minister, Emma Little-Pengelly (DUP) now share the leadership of the new Northern Ireland Government. This partnership will be pivotal in establishing the social and political conditions for sustainable peace in Northern Ireland:

> Michelle is an Irish republican and I am a unionist. We will never agree on those issues, but what we can agree on is that cancer doesn't discriminate and our hospitals need fixing.[5]

In 2007 the partnership between Ian Paisley and Martin McGuinness lasted a year and set an example of collaborative political leadership.

Both men came under significant pressure from their political colleagues for appearing to "like each other". The next First Minister was Peter Robinson (DUP) who worked with Martin McGuinness (Sinn Féin) as deputy First Minister between 2008 and 2016. Their relationship and leadership brought stability to the devolved government.

At the time of writing Michelle O'Neill and Emma Little-Pengelly have made history. Their first speeches were focused on urgent operational issues and both share a commitment to the future rather than revisiting the past. Stable government and sustainable peace now rest on the courage these women leaders have to work together to set an example for new forms of leadership to emerge in Northern Ireland politics.

Notes

1. Long, N. (2024) Stormont Institutions must be reformed to avoid future collapses, *The Irish News,* 30 January, p. 1.
2. McDonald, M. (2024) DUP agrees deal to revive Stormont, *Irish Republican News,* 30 January, p. 1.
3. O'Neill, M. (2024) Irish Republican News, 3 February, p. 1.
4. First speech to the Northern Ireland Assembly by Emma Little-Pengelly, mydup.com 3 February 2024.
5. *ibid.*

Abbreviations and political groups

APNI:	Alliance Party Northern Ireland formed in 1970 and as of 2024, the third largest party in government
Green Party NI:	This party was established in 2006 but maintains close links with Green Parties in England, Scotland and Wales
CLMC:	The Combined Loyalist Military Command, a grouping of loyalist paramilitary organisations including the UVF, the UFF, the UDA and the RCH
DUP:	The Democratic Unionist Party founded in 1971
DSD:	The Downing Street Declaration, 1993, was a joint Declaration between the British and Irish Governments
IRSP:	Irish Republican Socialist Party formed in 1974
MLA:	A Member of the Legislative Assembly, which is a body which passes laws and examines policy
MP:	In the UK a Member of Parliament represents their local constituency in parliament and can influence policy at the UK state level. In contrast MLAs have collective responsibility for state legislation and policy that affects the whole of Northern Ireland
New IRA:	A merger of RAAD, the Real IRA and independent republicans formed in 2012
NICRA:	The Northern Ireland Civil Rights Association formed in 1967

NIO:	The Northern Ireland Office, a department of the British Government responsible for Northern Ireland affairs. It is led by a Secretary of State with offices in London and Belfast. It was formed in 1972.
NIWC:	The Northern Ireland Women's Coalition, a cross-party coalition formed in 1996 who took part in peace talks in 1997–1998 and disbanded in 2006
OIRA:	The Official Irish Republican Army, a republican paramilitary organisation reluctant to get involved in the violence in Northern Ireland in 1969. Their politics was far-left and focused on ending partition
Peace People:	A peace organisation based in Belfast founded in 1976 by Máiread Maguire, Betty Williams and Dublin journalist Ciaran McKeown
PIRA:	The Provisional Irish Republican Army founded in 1969 and disbanded in 2005
PSNI:	The Police Service of Northern Ireland formed in 2001
PUP:	The Progressive Unionist Party linked to the UVF and the Red Hand Commando
RAAD:	Republican Action Against Drugs formed a vigilante group in 2006 who became part of the New IRA in 2012
Real IRA:	The Real IRA formed in 1997 and now part of the New IRA
Real UFF:	The Real Ulster Freedom Fighters founded in 2007 by ex UDA and UFF
RHC:	The Red Hand Commando, a small loyalist paramilitary group formed in 1972

RSF:	Republican Sinn Féin formed in 1986 in protest at the political strategies of Sinn Féin, which were deemed to be counter to traditional republican principles
RUC:	The Royal Ulster Constabulary formed in 1922 after the partition of Ireland and was replaced by the PSNI in 2001 under the terms of the Belfast/Good Friday Agreement
SF:	Sinn Féin, a political party in the Republic of Ireland and Northern Ireland. SF politicians as at 2024 hold a majority in the Northern Ireland Assembly
SDLP:	The Social Democratic and Labour Party formed in 1970
TUV:	Traditional Unionist Voice formed in 2007 after a split with the DUP
UDA:	The Ulster Defence Association, formed in 1971 to coordinate the activities of Protestant vigilante groups who ended their armed campaign in 2007
UFF:	The Ulster Freedom Fighters, a paramilitary group formed in 1973 by more militant members of the UDA
UUP:	The Ulster Unionist Party, a unionist party who were in government in governed Northern Ireland from 1921–1972
UVF:	The Ulster Volunteer Force, a loyalist paramilitary organisation formed in 1965 who ended their armed campaign in 2007 but continue to be involved in organised crime.

Political stakeholders (February 2024)

There is a spectrum of far-right-wing to far-left-wing politics in Northern Ireland which represent the traditional positions on sovereignty i.e. remain part of the UK versus the reunification of Ireland. However, the middle ground of politics is a space to watch. With an electorate experiencing health, social and economic pressures there is an expectation that politicians will now concentrate on urgent issues and focus on the best interests of the people of Northern Ireland. A summary of the main parties includes:

Unionist parties

- DUP: far-right
- TUV: far-right
- UUP: centre-right
- PUP: centre-left

Republican parties

- RSF: far-left
- IRSP: far-left
- Sinn Féin: centre-left to left wing

Nationalist and moderate parties

- SDLP: centre-left (*nationalist*)
- APNI: centre-centre-left (*non-sectarian*)
- Green Party: centre (*non-sectarian*)

Current ministers in the Northern Ireland Executive (February 2024)

- Caoimhe Archibald: Sinn Féin (*Finance*)
- Paul Givan: Sinn Féin (*Education*)
- Emma Little-Pengelly: DUP (*deputy First Minister*)
- Naomi Long: Alliance Party (*Justice*)
- Gordon Lyons: DUP (*Communities*)
- Andrew Muir: Alliance Party (*Agriculture, Environment and Rural Affairs*)
- Conor Murphy: Sinn Féin (*Economy*)
- John O'Dowd: Sinn Féin (*Infrastructure*)
- Michelle O'Neill: Sinn Féin (*First Minister*)
- Robin Swann: UUP (*Health*)

Other key players (February 2024)

- Chris Heaton-Harris: Conservative Party (*Secretary of State for Northern Ireland*)
- Mary Lou Madonald: Sinn Féin (*Opposition Leader in the Irish Government*)

- Rishi Sunak: Conservative Party (*Prime Minister of the United Kingdom*)
- Leo Varadkar: Fine Gael (*Taoiseach of the Irish Republic*)

Paramilitary organisations (active in 2024)

Loyalist: UDA, UVF, RHC and Real UFF
Republican: New IRA

Terms and places

Abstention: A Republican principle that prevents Sinn Féin politicians from taking seats in the British parliament and the Irish Dáil

AIA: The Anglo-Irish Agreement, 1985, a treaty between the UK and the Republic of Ireland to facilitate an end to "The Troubles"

Áontu: an all-Ireland party formed in 2019 and supportive of a united Ireland

Ard Fheis: The annual convention of a political party

Belfast City and religious segregation: west (mainly Catholic), east (mainly Protestant), north and south (a combination of both communities)

Belfast/Good Friday Agreement, 1998: This was a binding agreement to create the conditions to end the violence and build a lasting peace. It was structured in three strands:

- *Strand 1* established the Northern Ireland Assembly and the Northern Ireland Executive

- *Strand 2* created institutions to promote the formation of common policies across Northern Ireland and the republic of Ireland
- *Strand 3* established bodies and institutions to promote greater co-operation between the British and Irish Governments

Dáil: Parliament of the Republic of Ireland

Derry (or Londonderry): The second largest city in Northern Ireland with a majority Catholic population who continue to call the city "Derry". Protestants tend to call the city "Londonderry"

D'Hondt: A system of power-sharing in the devolved government in Northern Ireland. After a general election, the political party with a majority nominates the First Minister and the second largest party nominates the deputy First Minister. Ministerial positions in the Executive and membership of the Assembly are based on proportional representation

Downing Street Declaration, 1993: A joint declaration between the British and Irish

Governments and an important precursor to the Belfast/Good Friday Agreement in 1998

Easter Rising, 1916: A mobilisation of Irish nationalists to free Ireland from British rule

First Dáil Éireann: Sinn Féin won a majority in the UK General Election in 1918. In accordance with republican principles, Sinn Féin MPs abstained and formed their own parliament on 21 January 1919

Long Kesh: A prison, also known as the "Maze" just outside Lisburn, south west of Belfast. Both loyalist and republican prisoners were sent there until its closure in 2000

Loyalist: Individuals and groups in Northern Ireland loyal to the British Crown

Nationalist: Refers to a majority of Catholics or supporters of SDLP who support a united Ireland but do not endorse violence

Northern Ireland Protocol: A trade agreement that allowed Northern Ireland to stay in the EU single market and to keep an open border with the Republic of Ireland

Republican: Nationalists who view the partition of Ireland in 1921 as an illegal act by the British Government

Stormont: Parliament Buildings in the Stormont Estate area of Belfast and the seat of the Northern Ireland Assembly. The Northern Ireland Executive is located at Stormont Castle.

Taioseach: Irish Prime Minister

Ulster: These are the four traditional provinces in the North of Ireland and were comprised of nine counties before partition in 1921. Six counties became Northern Ireland and three counties became part of the Republic of Ireland

Unionist: Refers to people who wish to keep Northern Ireland within the UK

Windsor Framework, 2023: A trade agreement between the UK and the EU to ease customs checks on goods from Britain to Northern Ireland

Recommended reading

Atran, S. (2010) *Talking to the Enemy: Violent Extremism, Sacred Values, and What it means to be human,* London, Allen Lane, Penguin Group.
Cochrane, F. (2013) *Northern Ireland: The Reluctant Peace,* Yale University Press.
Cochrane, F. (2008) *Ending Wars,* Cambridge, Polity Press.
O'Doherty, M. (2023) *How to fix Northern Ireland,* London, Atlantic Books.
Fukuyama, F. (2018) *Identity: Contemporary Identity Politics and the Struggle for Recognition,* London, Profile Books.
Hedges, C. (2003) *War is a force that gives us meaning,* New York, PublicAffairs Books, Random House.
Mitchell, G. (1999) *Making Peace: The inside story of the making of the Good Friday Agreement,* London, William Heinemann.
Powell, J. (2014) *Talking to Terrorists: How to end armed conflicts,* London, Vintage Books, Penguin Random House.
Powell, J. (2009) *Great Hatred, Little Room,* London, Vintage Books, Penguin Random House.
Tonge, J. (1998) *Northern Ireland: Conflict and Change,* Essex, UK Pearson Education Ltd.
Taylor, P. (2023) *Operation Chiffon: The Secret Story of MI5 and MI6 and the Road to Peace in Ireland,* London, Bloomsbury Publishing.
Van De Kolk, B. (2014) The *Body Keeps the Score: Mind, brain and body in the transformation of trauma,* London, Penguin Random House.

DEFINITION
Vectors are not like typical academic monographs. They are aimed at a more general audience, which might include undergraduate students, academics working in other fields, practitioners, policymakers, and the public. They provide a platform for established academic authors to reach a larger audience than usual, or to speak to new audiences; to deliver bold new arguments; to write unencumbered by the usual obligations for referencing; and to be exciting, provocative and even polemical.

ALREADY PUBLISHED:
Massimo Arcangeli, *Genderless Grammar*.
Alberto Lucarelli, *Tradition & Revolution*.
Sally Watson, *Sustainable Peace in Northern Ireland*.

COMING SOON:
Simone Gozzano, *On Consciousness*.

www.ingramcontent.com/pod-product-compliance
Ingram Content Group UK Ltd.
Pitfield, Milton Keynes, MK11 3LW, UK
UKHW021323180426
11947UKWH00017B/1405